Solved:

How to Get More from Your LinkedIn Experience

Donald P. Roy, Ph.D.

To Sara, Chris, Sidney, and Ethan

Contents

Introduction

Do I need to go all in on LinkedIn?

You have been convinced that being on LinkedIn is good for you (or maybe you are still trying to convince yourself). Perhaps a social media-savvy friend told you about someone interesting he met on LinkedIn. Or, a former co-worker received an offer too good to refuse from another company that found her through her LinkedIn profile. Maybe you came to the realization that your LinkedIn presence needs improvement. Regardless of the source of inspiration, you want to step up your LinkedIn game. It could be the best decision you will ever make for building your personal brand.

A Social Network Forerunner

When you think about spending time on social media, LinkedIn probably is not top of mind. It is not as ubiquitous as Facebook, not as snarky as Twitter, and not aesthetically captivating as Instagram. Interestingly, Facebook, Twitter, and Instagram launched after LinkedIn, in 2004, 2006, and 2010, respectively. Reid Hoffman founded LinkedIn in 2003. The idea was to create a platform where professionals could network in pursuit of achieving business goals.

User growth on LinkedIn was steady in the early years and exploded in 2008 when it created a stronger global presence and launched French and Spanish versions of the site. LinkedIn's remarkable growth has continued. By 2018, LinkedIn's user base had grown to more than 560 million users worldwide, with more than 70% of users living outside the United States. The number of LinkedIn members pales in comparison to Facebook, but growth plans are ambitious. A long-range member goal for LinkedIn is three *billion*.

LinkedIn's user base is active, too. While LinkedIn does not release statistics on monthly active users, estimates of that figure are in the neighborhood of more than 100 million. The combination of LinkedIn's large global reach, active network, and growth potential make it too important to ignore.

What People Do on LinkedIn

Whether you already have a LinkedIn account or are just starting you may be unclear exactly how people spend their time on LinkedIn. User activity can be broken down into five categories:

- *networking-* meeting other people with shared interests
- *searching-* looking for a job (or looking to hire someone)
- *learning-* keeping current on news and trends
- *creating-* publishing original content
- *selling-* prospecting for clients and promoting business.

You may not engage in all five categories of activity, and even if you do, the amount of time you spend in each category varies by person and field. The aim is not necessarily to do all of these activities but to do the *right* activities that will create value for others while enhancing your personal brand.

How to Use This Book

The chapters that follow spotlight 25 different ideas to make LinkedIn work for you. You may be very comfortable implementing some ideas, unsure about others, and even dismissive of some ideas. That is OK because the net result will be a deeper understanding of LinkedIn and how to leverage it for your benefit. Each chapter includes a call to action to put an idea to work if you choose to pursue it.

Let's get started—more than half a billion people are waiting on us!

Part I: The Basics

1

Not Just another Social Network

Is LinkedIn necessary if I use other social networks?

Although we live in a world of rapid change, do not overlook one constant: We will never have more than 24 hours in a day. Time is one of our most precious resources. When new tasks or interests come along that will tap that fixed resource, we may be skeptical about something new draining time.

This dilemma could come into play for you when assessing the value of investing time on LinkedIn. Whether or not you already have a LinkedIn account, you will likely need to carve out time to immerse yourself and enhance your presence. You will not add value for others or receive value yourself by logging on every now and then. If you are like the average person, you already spend almost two hours a day on social media. You may be questioning whether you would have time to spend on LinkedIn or if time spent would be justified.

To address these concerns, contrast LinkedIn with three popular social networks: Facebook, Twitter, and Instagram. Can you realize the same benefits from these social networks for your personal brand that LinkedIn can deliver?

Facebook

If you are looking for the largest audience, there is no doubt that Facebook is the place to be with more than 2.2 billion monthly active users and counting. That said, reasons for using LinkedIn and Facebook differ in the following ways:

- Facebook relationships are based on social friendships. LinkedIn connections are based on professional relationships.

- Many Facebook users turn to the site for entertainment. LinkedIn users have business-related motives.

- Facebook is a place where users consume for personal enjoyment and benefit. Many users avoid mixing personal and business communication. LinkedIn is a channel that meets the need to create and consume work-related content.

LinkedIn has a clear position as a channel for professional communication. Facebook is more like an amusement park.

Twitter

Keeping up with news in your field is possible through Twitter. It is a very active channel, with more than 500 million tweets posted daily. Also, following news in real-time is one of Twitter's greatest strengths. However, Twitter has limitations compared to LinkedIn:

- Twitter has a 280-character maximum for posts. This limit hinders quantity of information conveyed in a single post.

- Twitter's standard relationship basis is "following." It is a weaker relationship than LinkedIn's standard of "connection." This difference is due to following is a one-way action (i.e., reciprocation not required). A LinkedIn connection is a mutual agreement to form a bond. LinkedIn also lets you choose to follow a user, similar to following someone on Twitter.

- Twitter is replete with parody and fake accounts. While some of them can be entertaining, they do not represent real people. LinkedIn has far fewer such accounts, meaning you are more likely connecting with real people.

Twitter can be a channel for self-learning, but it is not as effective for fostering personal relationships as LinkedIn.

Instagram

One of the fastest growing social networks has been Instagram. It launched in 2010 and now has more than one billion monthly active users. Like Twitter, Instagram users are active content creators, uploading nearly 100 million photos daily. Despite Instagram's broad appeal, there are limitations of its use for professional purposes. Among them are:

- Instagram content is limited to the visual channel (photos and video). Long-form text is not effective, and links to web pages cannot be easily placed in posts.
- Like Twitter, following another user is the basis of Instagram relationships (a one-way connection). Moreover, following other Instagram users can be challenging; as many 50% of all Instagram accounts may be private. This setting requires a user to approve followers.
- Instagram is a mobile-first platform. It is less versatile when using it on a desktop computer.

For professionals who create value and impact visually, Instagram can be a vital communication channel. Its strength as a visual channel is also a limitation as an exclusive social network for personal branding.

Act on It

Should you have a presence on LinkedIn, particularly if you already use other social networks? In nearly 100% of cases the answer is "yes." The main exception would be a person who has no need to establish and grow a professional network. You could probably make a list of occupations in which building a network is not important. You would be correct... assuming a person plans to work in that occupation for the duration of their working years.

Today's fluid world of work is one in which people change jobs 10-15 times during their career. Keep in mind networking is done more for the future than the present. While you may not feel like it is important to focus on networking now, remember that you are doing it for a time in the future when you could benefit from making connections with others. LinkedIn is an ideal channel for professional networking.

2

Getting Started

What should I do to (re)start a LinkedIn presence?

If you are a long-time LinkedIn user, you are past the stage of becoming familiar with LinkedIn's features. However, you might benefit from a refresher on LinkedIn basics. If you are new to LinkedIn or need guidance on establishing a presence, you will want to review these recommended first steps.

One of my favorite sayings when tackling a challenging goal is "the best way to eat an elephant is one bite at a time." The prospect of completing a major project can be overwhelming until you realize that by consistently doing small tasks you inch closer toward project completion. For example, a 200-page book could mean writing a 55,000-word manuscript. Creating a document that long would be daunting unless you break it down to 500 words daily. You will be finished in less than four months by making small strides.

The same approach will serve you well when managing your personal brand on LinkedIn. You will not get your LinkedIn presence to an ideal state the day you set up an account. If you compare the appearance of your account and number of connections to LinkedIn veterans, you might be embarrassed. Before you have those thoughts, remember that, like eating an elephant LinkedIn effectiveness occurs one bite at a time.

So what should you do to set the table to begin taking bites of LinkedIn? Start with the three tasks: claim your identity, connect with real life, and search, search, search.

Claim Your Identity

The first task you must complete after setting up an account (or coming back to your account after a period of inactivity) is adding information to the sections of your profile. Keep in mind your profile is the brochure for Brand You on LinkedIn. It is what others review to find out who you are and learn more about you.

The content in your profile is so vital to your LinkedIn success that several chapters examine different profile parts. Your profile is a work-in-progress regardless if you are a newbie or LinkedIn veteran. It stands to reason—you would not develop an ad or brochure for a product and never revise it. You tweak the message to respond to changes in customers, competition, and the product. Similarly, setting up your profile is not a one-and-done proposition.

When getting started, make sure you address these LinkedIn profile elements:

- *Photo.* Have a professional looking headshot of yourself. You are not a silhouette; upload a photo.
- *Headline.* At the very least, write a descriptive headline that tells people what you do (i.e., profession, job title, and organization). Your headline can be more impactful. Chapter 4 addresses writing an effective headline.
- *Summary.* The summary section of your profile should be a narrative that offers a glimpse into the value you offer.

It should not be a copy-and-paste of the experience section from your résumé. How to write a summary is the focus of chapter 5.

- *Experience.* This section of your profile is similar to the experience section of your résumé. Although you should highlight your experience in creative ways (which is covered in chapter 6), a good starting point is using the work experience summary written for your résumé.

Your LinkedIn profile contains other sections that need to building out, sooner rather than later. However, completing these four sections provides a basic profile that others can use to glean information about you in the meantime.

Connect with Real Life

Once you have set up your LinkedIn identity, connect with real-life friends and acquaintances to begin growing your professional network. In his book *The Power of Who*, executive search expert Bob Beaudine suggests we already know all the people we need to know. Thoughts of networking tend to focus on finding and meeting people we do not know. We already know scores of people from different corners of our life. A partial list of real-life connection sources includes:

- parents' friends
- siblings' friends
- neighbors
- fellow church congregants
- former teachers
- classmates
- bosses
- co-workers

OK, that is enough. I think you get the picture. You have made many face-to-face connections over the years. Do not discount the value of connecting with people you know in real life (IRL) on LinkedIn.

A next-door neighbor who works in a field completely unrelated to yours might appear to have little value as a connection. However, he could connect you with his aunt who holds the exact position you aspire to reach one day. You may never have known about the aunt if you did not connect with the neighbor. Not all IRL connections will have that kind of value on LinkedIn. Instead of trying to qualify the strength of those connections, just make them!

Search, Search, Search

The third step for getting your LinkedIn presence up and running is to begin complementing IRL connections. A precious space on LinkedIn holds the key to implementing this step: the search bar. When you enter a search term (e.g., person's name, company name, or job title), LinkedIn returns results in up to six categories:

- people
- jobs
- content
- companies
- groups
- schools

LinkedIn's search capabilities enable you to look for people and companies whom you already know, follow or make connection requests with companies or people you want to know, and find common people with common interests in groups.

Learn more about making the most of LinkedIn's search function in chapter 9.

Act on It

Whether you are new to LinkedIn or have had an account for some time, you will benefit by going through the three steps discussed here.

- Make sure your brand identity elements of photo, headline, summary, and experience are up-to-date and are a good representation of your brand value.
- Compile a list of real-life connections and search for them on LinkedIn. Connect with IRL connections; do not try to qualify their relevance to your profession or field.
- Use the search function to follow companies, follow or connect with people, and join groups to begin growing your network beyond IRL connections.

3

What to Do

How should I spend time when on LinkedIn?

Rome was not built in a day. Likewise, your personal brand will not be built to your satisfaction in one day. Maintaining a brand presence on LinkedIn is an ongoing task. It is not like painting a picture that is set forever once the paint dries. Instead, your painting on LinkedIn requires constant touch-ups.

A common question posed by less experienced LinkedIn users is how much time to spend on LinkedIn. The correct answer to that question is "it depends." If you are using LinkedIn strictly for job search, you will likely need to invest more of yourself than if your activity is primarily for professional networking. If LinkedIn is a source of leads for your business, you will use it more than job seekers or networkers.

A study of social media usage by the blog Socially Aware found that on average a LinkedIn user spent 17 minutes *a month* on the site—that is about 35 seconds a day. This characteristic of LinkedIn users is one for which being above average should be a personal priority. If only a brand could be built in a matter of seconds… but it cannot so carve out time to spend on LinkedIn.

Set a Time

It does not take much analysis to realize 35 seconds a day on LinkedIn will not cut it for brand building. Set a modest goal of one hour per week to engage with the LinkedIn platform. That level of activity would make you way above average, spending 250% more time using LinkedIn than the typical user. Time spent does not equal success, of course. However, you stand to accomplish much more in building your professional network than someone who logs on for just a few minutes a week.

Commit to visiting LinkedIn at a set time—every day, every other day—but not too infrequently. Scheduling the same time of day each time could simplify this obstacle. If 11:30 a.m. Tuesday and Thursday for 30 minutes is your LinkedIn time, you are less likely to forget to check in with what is happening in your network.

I do not claim to be a mind reader, but surely some of you read the last paragraph and thought to yourself "I am too busy to set aside a time for LinkedIn." Righhhht—you cannot add time to the day. If that is how you feel, reflect on your current media consumption. The same study that found LinkedIn users spend 17 minutes a month on the site found average monthly consumption of Facebook to be 6.75 hours. Netflix users spend an average of 10 hours a month streaming video. Even if your media consumption is below average, you likely could reallocate time to LinkedIn.

Top 10 List

If you are doing LinkedIn on a time budget, here are 10 essential actions you should perform regularly. The order is not crucial, and the time spent on the 10 actions will vary from week to week. The 10 actions fall into three categories: follow-up, networking, and learning.

Follow-Up

A starting point for a LinkedIn session is to do some housekeeping to check on correspondence and ensure your profile information is current.

1. Review any connection requests received and decide how to act on them (accept or ignore)
2. Check Messaging for any messages that you should answer
3. Review people you have met or with whom you interacted this week (in-person, online, e-mail, telephone). Search for them on LinkedIn. Send a personalized connection request reminding the person how you met and expressing why you would like to connect on LinkedIn.
4. Scroll through your profile and ensure it is up to date.

Networking

LinkedIn is a social networking site, so be sure that you devote ample time to networking. If that sounds too vague or even overwhelming, adopt this simple definition of networking: "building good relationships." Manage your professional network through a mix of nurturing existing relationships and exploring possibilities for new ones.

5. Acknowledge important events for your connections (e.g., work anniversary, new position, or birthday)
6. Offer something of value to your network; share an article or web page link, write an update, or celebrate successes of client, colleague, or your company
7. Check out the "People also viewed" section on your profile page for possible new connections; these people have similarities with you in some way

8. Scroll through "People you may know" section so you can identify people to whom you might want to send a connection request.

Learning

In addition to giving to others through networking activities, make time for yourself to learn and grow. Remember that others are creating and sharing content for your benefit just as you should strive to do. Take advantage of what is being published and consume.

9. Review your news feed to see content that has been posted, shared, and liked by connections on others you follow

10. Check out latest conversations in groups to which you belong (Groups are also a source of potential new connections).

Act on It

This one is simple: Do it! Whether you use LinkedIn for 60 minutes once a week, 30 minutes twice a week, or 10 minutes six times a week, consistently spend time there. Like so many other practices, spending time on LinkedIn is a habit... so is not spending time on LinkedIn. Resolve to be above average and spend at least one hour a week building good relationships.

4

Judge a Book by Its Cover

Why are headline and photo important?

We live in a world that is saturated with information, to say the least. While we are exposed to more stimuli, we still have the same 24 hours in a day. The increased efforts to reach us mean that attention is at a premium. One has but a few seconds to make an initial connection with an audience. We exchange attention for possible benefits.

The challenges of the Attention Economy work both ways. We have limited attention to give others, and we must deal with the limited attention others have when trying to sell ourselves and ideas. It is this latter situation that comes into play with the first elements of your personal brand people view on LinkedIn: your headline and profile photo. A scan of these two bits of personal information determines whether someone will devote attention to you or move on to the next profile.

Like the above-the-fold area of a newspaper or website can attract or lose audience members, you must capture attention of viewers who come across your LinkedIn profile. Relevant experience, education, or other qualifications may be overshadowed by a headline or photo that fails to gain attention.

Headline: More than Words

The first section of a LinkedIn profile is called the Intro. It contains basic information about you—name, current position, education, and location. One other section of text in the Intro is the headline. What is the purpose of the headline? It should capture attention and communicate value. It draws in the viewer for a longer look at the story that is your profile.

Keep in mind the following considerations when composing your profile headline:

- A headline can be a maximum of 120 characters. Experiment with different versions to utilize available space.

- Do not be too boring in your description. Avoid using a simple descriptor like "staff accountant" or "student." If you feel compelled to put your title or role in the headline, build on it by communicating your value. For example, instead of "Student at University of Tennessee," build interest with a statement like "Marketing Major | Future Sales Professional | Passion for Logistics."

- At the other extreme, avoid fluff words not supported with evidence. "Guru," "ninja," and "expert" rise to the top of the list of fluff terms. An exception to "expert" is if others refer to you as such. It is OK for others to deem you an expert; do not go there on your own.

- Avoid coming across as desperate... even if you are. Your headline should never read, "Looking for a job." Sell what you have to offer, not that you are unemployed.

- Do not include a telephone number in the headline. Ensure your contact information (including phone number) is current in your profile. Including it in your headline comes across as aggressive and forward.

Embrace composing a headline as a creative challenge and not a fill-in-the-blank exercise.

Picture Is Worth a Thousand Words

The words arranged to create a headline matter, but the visual impact of a profile photo cannot be overstated. Whether we realize it or not, we form beliefs and attitudes toward total strangers with no more than a quick glance at them. Reactions to a photo can include opinions about the person's intelligence, friendliness, collegiality, and more. One study of LinkedIn usage found looking at a user's profile photo accounts for 19% of time spent viewing a profile.

Given the influence your profile photo can have on others' judgments about you and building interest, practice the following guidelines for a profile photo.

- A profile photo should be at least 200 x 200 pixels; recommended size is 400 x 400 pixels.

- Use a professional-looking headshot. You need not spend a small fortune on a session with a professional photographer. Most smartphones today take quality photos. You will eventually want to upgrade your photo to one taken by a professional photographer. Be mindful of the setting and only use a photo that has a close-up view of you. It is probably not a good idea to use a random photo from your saved photos because it was not taken for the need at hand.

- Dress in a manner consistent with the audience (industry) to which you want to connect. If you are unsure how someone in your target audience dresses, ask a connection or trusted adviser like a teacher. You can also observe how others in your target field or industry appear in their profile photos.

- Use a photo of you... and only you. Do not crop a photo of you with someone else. That photo with a buddy's fingers draped over your shoulder or girlfriend's hair flowing behind your ear can be distracting.

- The worst photo for your profile? The default silhouette. Profiles with a photo are 11 times more likely to be viewed. Privacy concerns are understandable, but they should be weighed against the reason you are on LinkedIn in the first place: to sell yourself.

- Enhance the visual appeal of your profile by adding a background image. Dimensions of a background image should be at least 1000 x 425 pixels and no larger than 4,000 x 4,000 pixels. Doing so enables you to replace the default background image with one that reflects your personality or interests.

Brands invest a great deal of thought (and money) into photography that presents their products in an appealing manner. Similarly, do not be haphazard in using just any picture to be your profile photo.

Act on It

You want to make a good first impression on LinkedIn. A headline and photo that represent who you are and value offered can make the difference between getting noticed and being overlooked. Ensure these vital branding tools are working in your favor.

- Write two or three versions of a headline, following the guidelines given in this chapter. You can test each version to get a sense of how it is received (and how much you like it). Revisit your headline occasionally and question if it still accurately captures the value you offer.

- Review guidelines for a profile photo. If you do not have a photo uploaded to your profile, do so now. If you have a profile photo, does it make your profile more compelling to view, or is it merely part of the landscape? Like your headline, the profile photo should be evaluated periodically to ensure it is a visual image of you with which you are pleased.

5

Your Personal Brand Bio

What is a Summary, and how should I approach writing it?

You have taken care of the first impression elements of your LinkedIn profile (headline and photo). Now, you tackle one of the most crucial self-marketing pieces of the profile: the Summary section. Before sharing ideas for writing an effective summary, let us begin by clarifying what the summary section should not be: a copy-and-paste redux of your résumé. The LinkedIn profile summary and a résumé serve two different purposes. It is possible for anyone who comes across your profile to view your summary. In contrast, you can target the contents of a résumé to attract interest among people in a certain industry.

Once you realize creating a LinkedIn profile summary is different altogether from writing a résumé, you should embrace the task as a creative self-marketing challenge. As such, you enjoy leeway in how to position your personal brand and the value you offer.

Telling the Story of You

The characteristic of writing a profile summary being a creative challenge cannot be overstated. Among all other duties associated with marketing Brand You, add the title of chief copywriter to your list of responsibilities. You must communicate the value you provide to others. The maximum 2,000 characters of the profile summary is your chance to be creative in sharing who you are, what drives you, and what you have done.

Writing a profile summary is not a fill-in-the-blanks exercise. You decide how to gain the attention of the audience. Among the approaches for writing a summary are the following five ways. Whatever approach you take, use one with which you are comfortable and fits with your personal brand.

1. *Reveal your purpose.* This approach focuses on describing your mission, or what inspires you. You could even include a personal mission or purpose statement to show how your reason for being drives you.

2. *Shine a light on the real you.* Authenticity is a highly desirable personal brand characteristic. Some people misunderstand the point of personal branding; the goal is not create a caricature of your ideal self. Simply put, be you when constructing a summary for your brand.

3. *Show your personality.* People are attracted to others they find interesting or with whom they have something in common. Allow the real you to be come through in your summary. For example if you have a sense of humor, let it appear in the summary. Is it risky to infuse personality into your LinkedIn presence? No, because you are not for everyone… no matter how hard you try to play it down the middle and attempt to cast a wide net.

4. *Run the highlights reel.* Your summary can be a recap of what you have accomplished to date. Be sure to emphasize how the accomplishments added value for others. The aim is to accent your capabilities and their impact, not write a self-congratulatory essay.

5. *Straightforward is OK.* Your take on a personal summary could be a matter-of-fact overview of experience and current situation. There is nothing wrong with taking this approach to writing your summary, especially if a matter-of-fact style fits your personality.

These five approaches are not an exhaustive list of options for writing a profile summary. They represent a marked improvement over copy-and-paste from your résumé. It does not matter which approach you use as long as you take on writing the summary as a creative challenge.

Amplify Your Message

In addition to adopting a particular style for writing your profile summary, other considerations can make the difference between being noticed and getting lost in the clutter of other users' profiles.

- *Lead content matters.* Just as a newspaper or magazine article might show a few words of text before forcing readers to turn the page for more, LinkedIn teases users with limited visible summary content. LinkedIn desktop users see the first 220 characters of the summary; mobile users see only the first 92 characters. You must entice searchers to click to see more by gaining their attention with the first two lines of the summary.

- *Think keywords.* You may have heard of copywriters and bloggers including keywords in their work so that search engines find them. Add LinkedIn profile summary writers to that list! Your summary benefits from having keywords in it that tip off readers to your target job title or role.

- *Facts tell but stories sell.* One of the most limiting characteristics of a résumé is that reveals little about you. This characteristic might sound strange—after all, a résumé is a summary about you (experience, education, skills, awards, and contact information). Yet, a standard résumé template allows little room for engaging readers through a narrative about you.

Act on It

Think of the 2,000-character space available for your summary as being a blank canvas. Although it can be an intimidating prospect (like the feeling of having to write a report that is due tomorrow morning that you have not begun), accept the challenge of writing a summary that departs from the stale sounding overview that describes most résumés. Get past the blank canvas by doing the following:

- Choose one of the five approaches for writing a summary. Pick an approach with which you are comfortable. Then, start writing! If you are comfortable with more than one approach, then write different versions of a summary to see how they compare.

If you are about to embark on writing a summary for the first time, visit other users' profiles to check out how others have composed their summary. You may find a style used by someone else that you like and see as a fit with your personal brand.

6

Knowledge and Ability Meet

How should I present my work experience?

A point emphasized in chapter 5 was the summary section of your LinkedIn profile should not be a copy-and-paste restatement of your résumé. The same holds true for the Experience section, to an extent. Yes, the overview of work experience in your profile should contain similar information to that found in a résumé. However, the format and space allocation of the experience section in a LinkedIn profile allows for a different, more descriptive presentation of how you have applied knowledge and ability.

Experience Goals

Avoiding a repeat of work experience information on your résumé in the experience section of your profile is a simple suggestion to follow. Creating an overview of experience that departs from the look of a résumé can be easier said than done, however. If it needs to be different from a résumé, what should it look like? To answer that question, let us start with establishing what the experience section should do for you.

Keep three goals in mind about what this section of your profile can do for you.

- *Serves as your "greatest hits" compilation.* Instead of emphasizing tasks and duties performed (like most everyone else), highlight achievements from each position held. Job duties can be similar for a given position regardless of employer. What will be unique to you is what you did. How did you benefit customers? What impact did you have on your employer (e.g., save the company money or help launch a new product)? The format of a LinkedIn profile enables you to be more descriptive in sharing your greatest hits than you can on a résumé.

- *Conveys keywords.* You can influence who sees your profile by choice of words used to describe experience. Have as an aim for the experience section to position yourself for the area with which you want to be associated. Job titles can serve this keyword role, but not always. For example, the title of Marketing Associate is vague—what does someone in this job do? She might have significant social media marketing responsibilities, but you would never know it from the job title. Ensure wording of experience contains relevant words and terms to pique interest of the audience you want to attract.

- *Describes jobs and roles, not just jobs.* Another limitation of job titles can be that they do not fully describe your duties. Summary information about a job held on the traditional résumé is usually limited to title. Employers do not hire titles; they hire abilities! As you summarize each job held, ensure that you do not fall into the résumé trap of only listing job titles. List a job title and short description of the role you fulfilled in that position. Emphasize actions performed, not just responsibilities that read more like a job description than an overview of experience gained.

The Voice of Experience

Understanding the goals of the experience section will put you ahead of most LinkedIn users. Many profiles are copy-and-paste renditions of one's résumé. Enhance your personal brand position by embracing a different take and pursuing the three goals of the experience section. In order to meet these goals, put the following tactics into practice to give a voice to your work experience.

- *List titles and roles, not just titles.* Recall one goal for constructing the experience section is to complement job title with a brief description of your role. Why? A job title may be not fully capture the work you did. For example, if one position you held was ecommerce manager, people viewing your profile might have preconceived notions of the job. Unfortunately, their associations with the job might not match the work you actually did. Instead, listing title and role such as "ecommerce manager responsible for email marketing, social media, and operations" gives a clearer picture of the scope of the job... and it strategically inserts keywords. Position title has a 100-character maximum in the experience section; make use of it!

- *Lose the bullet points.* The first move should be to eliminate bullet points that likely are present in the experience section of your résumé. Do not ditch the content, just the bullets. How do you do that? For each job summarized, take up to three salient bullet points. Put the information conveyed in those bullet points in sentence form, pulling together the list items into a single passage.

- *Relate personal strengths to experience.* While it is important to summarize the role and accomplishments on the job, be sure to link what happened to personal strengths that made it possible. If you led a customer support that enjoyed a 15-point rise in customer satisfaction score, cite one or more strengths utilized to lead the team to higher performance. This practice combines the basic bulleted list on a résumé and the more descriptive personal attribute highlights often found in a cover letter.

- *Go beyond text.* Complement the written summary of experience in a position with images, documents, or links to relevant websites. LinkedIn allows you to upload many common file types for presentations, documents, and images. Adding other media gives additional information or even samples of your work. It also gives you an advantage over "competition" (others vying for the attention of the same audience). Many users are unaware you can add multimedia content to this profile section or simply choose a text-only presentation of experience.

You may be wondering if there are space constraints in the experience section. Yes, but at 1,000 characters per job listed, you should be able to easily create a richer description of experience than a résumé gives. In addition, the ability to upload multimedia content allows for presenting even more about your abilities for which character limit does not come into play.

Act on It

If you have a completed LinkedIn profile already, the experience section likely resembles a résumé. It is not an indictment against you or your LinkedIn skills (after all, you would not be reading this book if you knew this information). Transform the straightforward presentation of work experience in your profile by putting the goals and tactics shared into practice. If you are new to LinkedIn and the experience section is empty, you have a blank canvas with which to work.

A suggestion for working through this part if you are doing a profile overhaul: Prepare a draft of the new and improved experience section in a document file. It will allow you to edit and make changes to find a style and voice with which you were comfortable. Then, copy and paste the updated summaries of experience into your profile. In the meantime, the existing content in your experience section will suffice.

7

Proof Points

How do I utilize skills, endorsements, and recommendations?

The experience section of your profile discussed in chapter 6 summarizes work history. It is a record of what you have done, but it may not be a complete picture of your abilities. While past experience is an indicator of your value, work history alone does not reflect your potential impact. Three complementary sections of a LinkedIn profile are skills, endorsements, and recommendations. Use them to help tell the story of your brand's value.

Skills

Just as you list specific skills you possess on a résumé, the skills section of your profile is where you make known your abilities. The skills spectrum is broad; skills listed can be general (e.g., problem solving or public speaking) or specific (e.g., Adobe Photoshop or logo design). You can list up to 50 skills on your profile. The top three skills will show up unless "Show more" is clicked in this section.

List strongest or most relevant skills first when setting up this section. Skills will appear based on number of endorsements received. You can influence others giving recommendations by putting most important skills at top of the list (they may not make it all the way through your list of 50 skills, so make sure to lead with the skills for which you want to be endorsed).

One more point: Only list skills that you actually possess. Stretching the truth is all too common on LinkedIn, particularly in the Skills section. One study found that 55% of LinkedIn users admit to misrepresenting their skills in their profile. Lying about your skills could help you get noticed and maybe even land a job. In the long run, the truth will be revealed if you claim to possess skills that you do not possess. Then, you would have to create another lie on your profile to cover up that you were fired for lying about skills!

Endorsements

The list of skills included in your profile is amplified and grown through endorsements. Other LinkedIn users can go to your profile and endorse you for specific skills. Users who view your profile can scan your list of endorsed skills for a quick read on your interests and abilities. The number of endorsements received for a skill appears next to a skill in your profile. As the number of endorsements for a skill increase, you build up social proof about the skills you possess through the validation of others.

Follow two simple practices for endorsements to have greater impact on your profile. First, the surest way to receive endorsements is to give them. The norm of reciprocity compels many people to return the favor after you endorse them. Second, take a moment to thank someone who gives you an unsolicited endorsement. Send a message acknowledging the endorsement to the endorser using LinkedIn's messaging feature. It is also good practice for keeping in contact with your network.

You may now realize that it is easy to give and receive endorsements. This characteristic is both a blessing and curse. Others can acknowledge your abilities with a few clicks—the convenience is a blessing. The curse is that some users turn endorsements into a game, looking to rack up as many endorsements as possible by liberally making endorsements. This behavior leads many LinkedIn users (including recruiters) to be skeptical about the value of endorsements appearing in a profile.

Recommendations

A recommendation is a more meaningful acknowledgement of your value than an endorsement. Someone who writes a recommendation for your LinkedIn profile takes the time to articulate your strengths. A recommendation can be powerful because it is permanent; it remains on your profile for as long as you want it there.

You may request first-degree connections to write a recommendation for you. If you ask a connection to write a recommendation, include in your request an explanation of why you seek a recommendation. You can even suggest points to include in the recommendation. A first-degree connection can also write an unsolicited recommendation. You choose whether you want to accept the recommendation so that it will appear on your profile.

If you are seeking recommendations, strive to get at least one recommendation for every job listed in the experience section. Also, recommendations from former teachers or professors give another perspective on your abilities. A rule to follow when asking for recommendations is to only ask people who know you and are familiar with your strengths. A college professor who taught you 10 years ago may have been one of your favorite teachers, but if you have not stayed in contact she may not even remember you, let alone be able to write a recommendation on your behalf.

The norm of reciprocity also applies to recommendations. One way to motivate someone to write a recommendation for you is to recommend that person first.

Act on It

The skills, endorsements, and recommendations sections of your profile are important for making the case for the value you offer. Ensure that all three sections work to sell you.

- Review the skills you have listed. Does the list reflect skills you possess? If you are unsure what skills to add, a helpful resource is LinkedIn's skills directory (https://www.linkedin.com/directory/topics/). Clean up your skills list by deleting any outdated skills or skills for which you were endorsed but do not want in your profile.

- When reviewing your skills list, click on each skill to see who endorsed you for that skill. If you have not endorsed that person for any skills, take a moment to reciprocate and endorse them.

- Identify a first-degree connection (e.g., current or former boss, former teacher, mentor, or co-worker) for whom you would feel comfortable writing a recommendation. Write a recommendation for that person. It will appear on their profile under recommendations received and on your profile under recommendations given. To write a recommendation, click More underneath a person's profile headline and select Recommend.

- Compile a list of first-degree connections such as a current or former boss, former teacher, mentor, or coworker who you would be comfortable asking to write a recommendation for you. To make the request, click More underneath the person's profile headline and select Request a Recommendation.

8

Get Set

Which account and privacy settings should I review?

Like any social networking site, you have some control over the user experience on LinkedIn. However, this control is meaningless if you do not take advantage of it. Users have varied motivations or benefits sought from being on LinkedIn. Some users are in the midst of a job search. Other users rely on LinkedIn for generating new business opportunities. Yet other users merely want to have a presence and engage in networking.

Thankfully, LinkedIn does not deliver a one-size-fits-all experience. Customize how other users and LinkedIn itself interacts with you by reviewing account and privacy settings. To get to there, click the drop down arrow beside Me in the banner at the top of the home page (desktop platform). Then select Settings & Privacy under the Account section. When using LinkedIn's mobile platform, access settings and privacy options by clicking the settings icon (gear image) to the right of the search bar. Customize your experience by reviewing settings in three categories: account, privacy, and communications.

Account Settings

The account settings area is for managing general aspects of your LinkedIn account. If you need to add or change an email address or change the account password, go here. Two settings in this area that you will want to check out are how your general information appears and news feed preferences.

- *General contact information.* Review the email addresses and phone numbers associated with your account. It is in this area that you can change your password should the need arise.

- *Feed preferences.* Customize your news feed by selecting people and companies to follow from LinkedIn recommendations by topic or area.

Privacy Settings

The Privacy tab has the largest number of options that enable you to strike a balance between openness and privacy for LinkedIn activity. The eleven settings mentioned here is not an exhaustive list of options, but they are among the most important and ones you probably wish to address.

- *Edit your public profile.* You can choose to let everyone see your public profile or no one see it. You can opt to make your entire profile visible or select specific sections to show.

- *Who can see your connections.* The choices are 'only you" and "your connections." While you may have personal reasons why you would not want others to view your connections, making connections visible to people in your network encourages networking. You stand to benefit by seeing connections of your first-degree connections; consider reciprocating that benefit to your network.

- *Viewers of this profile also viewed.* This setting determines if profiles of users with similar profile characteristics will appear on beside your profile page when it is viewed. Users appearing in this space usually are a mix of first-degree and second-degree connections. You have the option of turning off this feature, but leaving it on could expose you to some potential connections.

- *Sharing profile edits.* Setting this feature to "yes" will alert your network whenever you make changes to your profile, make recommendations, or follow companies. If you do not want others to know of certain activity such as updating your profile as part of a job search, then set this feature to "no."

- *Notifying connections when you're in the news.* Spread the word when you are mentioned in posts or articles by setting this feature to "yes." It is a way to let others indirectly sing your praises.

- *Who can see your last name.* First-degree connections will always see your full name. However, you can maintain some privacy by opting to let non-connections see first name, first initial of last name only (e.g., Don R.). Unfortunately, LinkedIn is not exempt from stalkers and creeps who use social media for inappropriate purposes. This option gives you some measure of privacy.

- *Followers.* Control who sees public updates you make by selecting "everyone on LinkedIn" or "your connections."

- *Blocking.* You may choose to keep people from interacting with you on LinkedIn. The option to block a user is found by clicking on "More" below a user's profile head-line (desktop platform) or the three dots below a user's profile headline (mobile platform) and selecting "re-port/block." You can review your list of blocked users and unblock users if you wish.

- *Unfollowed.* If there are connections whose updates you do not wish to see in your news feed but do not want to sever the connection, choose to unfollow them. The op-tion to unfollow a connection is found by clicking on "More" below a user's profile headline (desktop plat-form) or the three dots beside a user's profile photo (mobile platform) and selecting "unfollow." You can follow the connection again later by clicking on the same area and selecting "follow."

- *Sharing profile when applying for a job.* You have the option of letting a job poster view your profile upon applying for a job through LinkedIn. Setting to "yes" gives your personal brand greater exposure beyond the job applica-tion… just make sure your profile is up-to-date and ef-fectively sells you.

- *Let recruiters know you are open to opportunities.* Keep in mind that recruiters are among the most active LinkedIn users, searching for talent to fill positions. If you are open to receiving pitches from recruiters, select "yes." Set this feature to "no" if you have no interest in receiving in-quiries about jobs for which you are not a prospect.

Communications Settings

Finally, review choices you have concerning communica-tion about connections, opportunities, and general messages from LinkedIn. A barrage of emails from LinkedIn, regardless of subject, could be a turnoff to using the site. Avoid the possibility of notification fatigue by reviewing settings for the types and frequency of email received from LinkedIn.

- *Email frequency.* LinkedIn wants to alert users about several types of interactions related to an account. Among the events that can trigger an email notification include:
  - Invitations
  - Messages sent through LinkedIn's messaging feature
  - Notifying connections when you join a group
  - Connections updates
  - Group updates
  - Jobs and opportunities
  - Messages from LinkedIn

You can select to receive emails for each of these triggers. If you opt to receive emails, another decision is the frequency you want to receive them. For some triggers like an invitation to connect with another user, you may want to receive an email when the event occurs. For other triggers like connections in the news, a weekly digest of activity might be sufficient.

Act on It

If you have never reviewed account and privacy settings or cannot remember the last time you did, now is a good time.

- Review the settings categories discussed in this chapter—account, privacy, and communications. Check current setting for each item. Make changes as desired depending on your goals (e.g., expand number of connections, find a job, or keep in contact with existing personal connections). Remember, if your situation changes (e.g., you suddenly find yourself looking for a job), revisit settings to ensure they work for, not against, you.

9

Crack the Search Code

What are ways to search for people, companies, or jobs?

LinkedIn's user base of more than 560 million people is at the same time impressive and daunting. The number of users is evidence of the potential to connect with friends and strangers alike. The challenge is how to sift through the massive amount of people, companies, posts, groups, and jobs to make relevant and meaningful connections. You can go it alone and sort through results delivered from LinkedIn searches to find who or what you seek. Alternatively, you can make the search process easier by applying filters or search commands for more precise results.

Several aspects of search on LinkedIn changed with an updated user interface in early 2017. If you are a relatively new LinkedIn user, you may have no idea how to perform searches beyond making an entry in the search bar. Let's go over search basics and how to make the most of LinkedIn's search features.

Search Basics

The search bar is easy to find on desktop and mobile platforms. Desktop users find the search bar at the top left on each page within navigation areas (Home, My Network, Jobs, Messaging, Notifications, and Me). Mobile users find the search bar located across the top of each page. Search results delivered are people with attributes most similar to the search term.

Results shown on the screen are "Top" results, but results delivered actually appear in seven categories. In addition to Top results, other categories are:

- People
- Jobs
- Posts
- Companies
- Groups
- Schools

A basic search often meets your needs, especially if you know exactly who or what you are searching to find. If you are looking for a person named Erica Jackson you met at a networking event who is in the same city as you and is a human resources manager at United Plastics, a quick look at search results should be all you need to find the Erica you wish to find out of more than 400 people with that name. The right Erica Jackson is more likely to surface in search results if she is a second-degree connection. That is, she and you have mutual connections but are not connected with each other.

Search Tips

Basic searches are fine if you have a good idea who or what you would like to find, but what if you want to find people based on certain characteristics? You are trying to find people, jobs, or companies based on certain search criteria. It is unknown who or what you will find; you only know that you who or what you want to find based on desired characteristics.

- *Focus your searches by using field commands.* They give direction to search, filtering the vast number of LinkedIn profiles to help you find people, companies, jobs, posts, groups, or schools. Field commands for narrowing search include:
  - o title:
  - o company:
  - o school:
  - o firstname:
  - o lastname:

- *Use quotation marks around search term for greater precision.* Search results returned will include any record that contains the search term. For a multi-word search, some results could be irrelevant to your search. When I enter a search for my undergraduate alma mater, search results could include any of the three words. I want to get search results that are a 100% match. Instead of entering the search:
  - o school: Mississippi State University

A more efficient results comes from this search:
  - o school: "Mississippi State University"

The first search returns results containing variations of any of the three words in the search term. The second search delivers only results that include the school name Mississippi State University.

- *Combine or exclude search elements by using Boolean search.* A staple of search engines is a Boolean search. This technique enables a searcher to perform a search using multiple terms to get more precise results. The operators AND, OR, and NOT can refine a search. For example, a search related to social media marketing can be more effective by using a Boolean search:

○ "social media" AND "community manager"

This search would return results containing the exact terms "social media" and "community manager."

○ "social media" OR "community manager"

This search would return results containing either the term "social media" or "community manager."

• *Apply search filters for clarity.* LinkedIn enables search refinement through nine search filters that can be applied individually or in combination to pinpoint search results. A basic search can be refined by using these filters. If you prefer an easier way to refine searches, LinkedIn makes that possible, too. When search results appear, a search filter menu appears to the right of the results list.

Filter results by any of the following variables:

○ Name
○ Connections (select 1st, 2nd, or 3rd degree)
○ Keywords (first name, last name, title, company, school)
○ Locations
○ Current companies
○ Past companies
○ Industries
○ Profile language
○ Nonprofit interests
○ Schools

Remember that these filters cannot be applied until after a search is entered whereas search commands and Boolean operators are used when you have search parameters in mind before searching.

- *Save searches for updates.* Save a search by clicking Create Search Alert. This button is located on the right side of the search results page beneath the search filters (desktop platform). Look for the heading Saved Searches. When you save a search, you can opt to receive daily or weekly email updates and notifications about that search.

Act on It

Search will help you connect with existing contacts and friends and lead you to people you do not know who have shared interests or characteristics (e.g., alumni of same college). Search results come in six different categories, and you can drill down deeper by applying one or more search filters to results.

This Act on It is straightforward—start searching! Utilize LinkedIn's search capabilities by performing searches as well as refining searches with search tips given in this chapter. Don't wait for other people to come to you; grow the network you desire through the power of LinkedIn search.

10

See and Be Seen

What ways can users find my profile through LinkedIn search?

One of the greatest benefits of LinkedIn is that it enables you find people and establish relationships with them. A future colleague, boss, mentor, or customer is out there; what a shame it would be if your paths did not cross. If you see yourself as a networking wallflower lacking confidence to meet new people, this characteristic of LinkedIn could be intimidating. Let us not forget LinkedIn is a *social* network. Thus, we should be open to social interactions.

Fortunately, the LinkedIn user experience is designed in ways to lead you to others… and lead others to you. Two elements of the user experience that you can use to your advantage and grow your network are data revealing who is viewing you and search settings to control how much information from your profile is visible when others search you.

Who is Viewing You

A dashboard summarizing recent activity shows the reach of your profile among other LinkedIn users. To see Your Dashboard, click: Me > View Profile (desktop platform) or click your profile photo at the top of the screen (mobile platform).

Below your headline and summary is "Your Dashboard." It shows three metrics:

- *Profile views.* You can learn who viewed your profile and how they got to it with this metric. Free account users see a limited number of results; premium users get full results on who viewed your profile.

- *Post views.* The reach of your posts is reflected in the post views metric. You will see a list of your posts and number of times each one appeared in others' news feed. Clicking the post views icon reveals summary data on viewers by organization, job title, and location.

- *Search appearances.* This metric shows the number of times your profile appeared in search results in a recent seven-day period.

Insights revealed by profile views, post views, and search appearances can be both interesting and flattering. However, vanity is not overarching goal for reporting these metrics. People are looking for you and exposed to your content. Knowing who they are can lead you to meeting new people and strengthening relationships with existing connections. These opportunities are possible by mining data reported on the dashboard.

Search Settings

Privacy settings that affect what others see from your profile (covered in chapter 8) give you control over personal information. Seeking level of privacy desired while having a presence on a public social network can seem counterintuitive to using social media. However, legitimate reasons exist for not wanting to be totally transparent with information from your profile. For example, reluctance to share is understandable if you ever have had personal information compromised online.

Two considerations for applying privacy settings that influence search are how visible you want profile information to be and how important growing your professional network to personal branding or career goals.

- *Profile viewing options.* Decide how visible you want to be when others see you have searched their profile. Options are:
    - o Name and headline (including profile photo)
    - o Profile characteristics- job description and organization (e.g., mine would be "University Professor at Middle Tennessee State University").
    - o Private mode- When using this setting, your information appears as "Anonymous LinkedIn user."
- *Growing a network.* The privacy setting "Viewers of this profile also viewed" controls whether profiles of other users see other LinkedIn users searched by people who search for you. In some situations, you may want to turn off this feature if you fear competitors will appear alongside your profile. Otherwise, consider this feature a service to help potentially expand one's professional network. They could be prompted to connect with someone they do not know (or forgot they knew) but with whom they have an interest in making a connection.

Act on It

Chances are you do not want to be invisible on LinkedIn. If your goal is to build a larger, richer professional network, take advantage of data and settings that can lead to new connections.

- Access the Your Dashboard feature. Review data on profile views, post views, and profile appearances in search results. If you have a free account, you will have less specific data on who these users are than if you have a premium account. Regardless, dashboard data give a glimpse of other LinkedIn users who likely have some interest in you.

Reach out to non-connections by following them or send an introduction message. Make contact with existing connections based on what you learn from dashboard data. Their viewing your profile could be a signal that something has changed with them. Take the opportunity to catch up.

11

Expense versus Investment

Do I need to pay for a LinkedIn Premium account?

If you are a user of prominent social networking sites like Facebook, Instagram, Twitter, or Pinterest, you are accustomed to everything being free. You are not required to pay for any of the features offered by these sites. In contrast, LinkedIn has free and paid accounts. Approximately 80% of users have a free account, so it is very possible that a free account can meet your objectives for using LinkedIn. With rates for premium accounts ranging from $29.99 to $99.95 per month for a 12-month commitment, comparing benefits offered by different premium accounts is warranted.

Free LinkedIn

You should default to having a free account. If you are new to LinkedIn or have not used your account extensively, take time to become more proficient at using LinkedIn's free features. Then, consider whether additional features not available to free account holders is worth the expense of switching to a paid account.

LinkedIn touts the following features for a free account:

- Build your professional identity on the web
- Build and maintain a large trusted professional network
- Find and reconnect with colleagues and classmates
- Request and provide recommendations
- Search for and view profiles of other LinkedIn members
- Receive unlimited InMail messages
- Save up to three searches and get weekly alerts on those searches.

The primary purpose for using a free account according to LinkedIn is to "create and maintain a professional profile online."

If you have no specific objective or if you want to utilize LinkedIn as Facebook for business, a free account will probably be sufficient. You will be able to interact with connections, meet new people, join and participate in groups, and engage in general networking without paying for an account.

Premium Account Options

Paying for a social media account could be a turnoff for some people to upgrade to a premium account. Your reasoning might be that you are not forced to pay to use any other social networking site; why should LinkedIn be any different? And, depending on what you want to accomplish on LinkedIn, such reasoning may be appropriate. However, becoming a premium account holder could prove to be a prudent investment if you have more ambitious business objectives for using LinkedIn.

Give LinkedIn credit for segmenting the market for premium accounts. The premium account options are segmented based on users' roles and objectives. Four premium account types from which you can choose are:

- *Job search.* Premium Career. $29.99 a month when billed annually. Gets 3 InMail messages. Access to online video courses. Preferred applicant means you move to top of recruiters' applicant lists.
- *Business.* Premium Business. $47.99 a month when billed annually. Gets 15 InMail messages. Access to online video courses, learn how you compare to other job applicants, get salary information. Unlimited browsing of first-and second-degree connections.
- *Sales.* Sales Navigator. $64.99 a month when billed annually. Gets 20 InMail messages. Lead Builder and Lead Recommendation features help users find decision makers. Unlimited browsing of first-and second-degree connections.
- *Talent.* Recruiter Lite. $99.95 a month when billed annually. As the name suggests, this premium account type is intended for professionals looking to hire employees. Career, Business, and Sales Navigator accounts are geared toward outreach for business opportunities. Recruiter Lite gives hiring managers unlimited people browsing and a platform for managing a candidate pool.

Deciding whether to spend money on one of these premium account types or simply maintain a free account could come down to viewing the decision as an expense or investment. You may have many other uses for $360 to $1,200 a year and believe free account features meet your needs. However, if spending $65 a month for a Sales Navigator account leads to sales opportunities worth thousands of dollars in incremental revenue, is it really an expense? If there is sufficient return on investment for paying for a LinkedIn account, a premium account could be a wise choice.

Act on It

You may have never considered a premium LinkedIn account, but you owe it to your professional brand to weigh premium account benefits to the cost of having those benefits.

- Review the four types of premium accounts. Identify which type would have the most relevance to your situation. Then, compare features you enjoy with a free account to features offered by the premium account type identified. Would additional benefits offered by a premium account (e.g., more access to potential employers or clients) be worth the expense?

- If you are wrestling with whether a premium account is worth it, take LinkedIn up on its offer to try a premium account for one month for free. It is a risk-free way to evaluate a premium account and decide if it is for you.

Part II: Networking

12

Build Good Relationships

What is networking, and how can LinkedIn help me network?

In Part I, the term "networking" appeared many times. We hear encouragement such as "build a network," "engage in networking," and of course, "use LinkedIn for networking." The advice flows freely and frequently; what often does not come with it is guidance on the why and how of networking.

Part II addresses several questions about making the most of the networking benefits LinkedIn offers. First, let's make something clear—what networking is. Simply put, the aim of networking is to build good relationships. It is a simple yet powerful view on what networking activities should accomplish. For anything you do in the name of networking, consider the criterion of whether it fosters building good relationships. If no, it is probably not networking.

The road to building good relationships can be full of obstacles. Interestingly, we put most of the obstacles in our own path. Namely, those obstacles are fears about networking. Do not be intimidated by this challenge. The obstacles to networking created by our fears can be managed through two steps: 1) Recognizing networking fears and 2) overcoming those fears.

Recognize Networking Fears

The existence of networking fears is not a matter of if they exist, but rather the degree to which fear impedes networking. In extreme cases, fear keeps people hanging out more in the restroom than the meeting area or worse, keeps them at home on their living room sofa. Many fears can be cited as obstacles to networking, but most of them can be classified as one of three worries:

- *I won't be liked.* Striking up a conversation with strangers can be daunting. Ever walk into a room and seemingly everyone is engrossed in conversation? Everyone except you, that is. Can I make a good first impression that will move people to like me, not shun me?

- *I won't be accepted.* You may feel that people can tolerate you in a brief interaction, but a brief encounter does not equal getting buy-in from others. But, if you focus on how you can create value for others you go a long way toward gaining acceptance. Why? You have made interactions with others about them, not you.

- *I won't be valued.* Even if I get past the mental barrier of feeling accepted, will I have anything to offer that makes others appreciate my value? Of you course you do, but that barrier makes it difficult for you to see.

Networking fears can be intensified for introverts. Concerns about being liked, accepted, and valued and are magnified for those of us who find it difficult to build rapport with people we do not know. Introverts must work harder to understand our networking fears and realize we are not much different than everyone else about our feelings toward networking.

Overcome Networking Fears

Understanding that networking fears are normal is an initial step toward becoming more comfortable with networking. Your outlook toward networking can minimize apprehension and transform networking from a chore to a strength of your brand. Become proactive about networking by putting the following steps in action:

- *Have a plan.* Don't just show up at a networking event. Do research on who will be there. Another aspect of planning is having an objective in terms of number of new people to meet or specific attendees you want to meet.

- *Make a good first impression.* Put yourself in other people's shoes— if you were them, would you want to spend time in conversation with you? Smile, make eye contact, and take a genuine interest in others. Otherwise, you may unwittingly send a message of being closed off from conversations.

- *Listen.* Your value to others depends heavily upon knowing their story, dreams, and needs. You will know none of that unless you commit to listening to them. Focus on the other person (not what you plan to say next) in order to understand them and how you might be of value.

- *Step out of your comfort zone.* You may feel that networking requires you step out of your comfort zone. Even if you are not terrified at the prospect of engaging strangers in conversation, you must make yourself open to growth by not limiting yourself to spending time with people you know already.

Change your outlook on networking to focus on the benefits. Networking is an efficient means of meeting new business prospects and a social aspect in that you can meet new people.

Act on It

Rather than allowing networking fears to hold you back from meeting new people, consider the how networking can become a personal strength. Implement the two steps of understanding networking fears and overcoming them:

- Engage in candid self-reflection about your attitude toward networking. If you have fears about networking, what are they? How do these fears limit effectiveness of your networking efforts?

- Think about someone you know who is an effective networker. What traits or practices contribute to his or her networking success? If you selected one trait or practice that person employs and adopted it to improve your own networking, what would it be? Why?

13

Making Connections

How can I increase chances of having connection requests accepted?

The practice of networking entails two types of activities: building and nurturing. In order to network, you must have people with whom to interact. Building activities relate to adding people to your network. Nurturing activities are relationship maintenance, interactions you have with connections once they are in your network.

Building and nurturing activities are similar to two types of customer-based marketing strategies: acquisition and retention. Acquiring new people in your network is building. Nurturing relationships with connections over time is a form of retention marketing. You must build and nurture to be an effective networker.

Let's take on the first of the two networking activities to better understand how to increase chances of having LinkedIn connection requests accepted. A disclaimer before we proceed: Suggestions offered here will work, but they do not have a 100% success rate. Know that in most instances when connection requests are not accepted, it is not you—it's them. The person declining your connection request has beliefs or issues holding them back more than rejecting something about you.

What to Say

The old saying "you only have one chance to make a good first impression" applies to making LinkedIn connection requests. The wording of a connection request (along with key profile elements photo and headline) either sells someone on clicking Accept or wondering why they should connect with you. Be convincing or be lonely!

One word should guide your network building activities on LinkedIn: why. Leave no doubt in the other person's mind why you want to connect and how it could potentially benefit them.

Avoid using LinkedIn's standard connection request message as the explanation for your why—it is weak. Do not use this statement as a stand-alone message to build your network:

"I'd like to add you to my professional network on LinkedIn."

The statement may be true, but it lacks a personal touch.

Tell the person whom you are inviting to connect why you have an interest in adding him or her to your network. You probably would not greet someone for the first time with "hi, I'm Alex. Let's be friends." Similarly, do not let your first interaction with someone on LinkedIn be the impersonal statement "I'd like to add you…" A connection request not be the first interaction you have with a person. It should follow an in-person meeting, after a phone call, or following an email exchange.

If you are wondering if it is appropriate to send a connection request to someone who you do not or barely know, the answer is "yes." However, clearly explaining why you want to connect is even more important in these situations since the other person is unfamiliar with you.

What to Do

A clear message explaining why you want to add someone as a connection goes a long way toward successfully growing your network. You can further increase the odds of building efforts by doing the following:

- *Pick the low-hanging fruit.* Connect with people you know offline (e.g., friends, relatives, co-workers, and classmates). It adds to your LinkedIn network quickly and potentially leads to adding some of their second-degree connections. In addition, making connections from real life could boost confidence in networking on LinkedIn if you are new or inexperienced user.

- *Be a person.* Include a photo in your profile. You know it already, but the large number of silhouette profile photos makes it worth stating one more time.

- *Connections beget connections.* Potential connections will consider the size of your network (i.e., number of connections you have) when deciding if they will accept your connection request.

- *Follow up.* Whether you are the inviter or invitee, follow an accepted connection request by thanking the other person. If you are the inviter, acknowledge their agreement to connect. If you are the invitee, thank the person for accepting and express interest in interacting now that you are connected.

Act on It

If you sit back and wait for people to invite you to network on LinkedIn, you could find yourself feeling like a wallflower.

Networking is not a spectator sport; get in the game by proactively building your LinkedIn network. Do your building efforts need refining? Work on making connection requests by doing this challenge:

- Think of someone you met recently, either in-person or online. Search for that person on LinkedIn. Assuming they have a LinkedIn account, send a connection request. Remind the person who you are, how you met, and why you want to connect on LinkedIn. Don't try this just once; it is likely to work so repeat as you meet new people.

14

Stranger Danger?

How do I handle interactions with people I do not know?

The nature of relationships on LinkedIn differs from social interactions on other social networking sites like Facebook and Twitter. Many people limit Facebook friends to people they already know in some way. The two-way nature of being someone's Facebook friend requires a user to accept another user's request for a connection to occur. In contrast, following someone on Twitter does not require reciprocation. As long as a user's tweets are not protected, following someone is as easy as walking through an open door.

The standard relationship between LinkedIn users is akin to Facebook friendship. Making a connection with another LinkedIn user requires that person accept an invitation to connect. Otherwise, the social tie is not made. Growing one's professional network is a worthy goal, but how can we build a network beyond people we already know? Networking requires stretching our comfort zone sometimes to reach out to people we do not know but with whom we would like to establish a relationship. In other words, we have to talk to strangers (and be open to strangers talking to us).

Interacting with people you know is one thing; initiating a relationship with a stranger can be far more uncomfortable. In this chapter, we look at each side of initiating a relationship with strangers: a) as the person receiving a connection request, and b) as the person making the request. The aim is to reduce anxiety about the initial exchange with someone you do not know. New connections and friendships may be just a click away.

Receiving Requests

Perhaps the type of message you will get most often on LinkedIn is a notification that another user wants to connect. Within a matter of seconds, we process the user's name, headline, and profile photo and draw conclusions. Among the first reactions might be:

- "I worked with this person"
- "She is a good friend of my colleague"
- "Who in the world is this guy?"

The third response is where we will focus. You have received a connection request from a stranger. Some LinkedIn users have a firm policy of ignoring requests from people they do not know. While this view can be understood and respected, it is possible to miss out on adding valuable connections to your network.

Networking on LinkedIn does not mean you should accept every connection request received. When a stranger requests to connect, probe further in an attempt to find out who the person is and more importantly, why he or she wants to connect. Take the following steps as you go through this process:

- *Check them out.* Begin by reading the person's profile, looking for shared connections, employers, education institutions, and LinkedIn groups. The other person has undoubtedly seen something intriguing in your profile.

Review their profile to see where you have common ground.

- *What is their why?* If a connection request from a stranger does not include a message explaining the request, ask the person why he or she made the request by sending a reply message to the connection request. You will find most connection requests are not tailored and thus, do not contain an explanation as to why the person wants to connect. There may be good reason you should accept, but it is OK to make them articulate the reason.

- *Judge a book by its cover.* A LinkedIn user's profile gives you a glimpse into who they are. An incomplete profile raises red flags about the user's potential quality as an addition to your network. Be wary of connection requests from people who do not have a profile photo. It is possible it is a fake account, but usually it is a person who does not understand how to use LinkedIn for networking and building a personal brand. As you look at the profile, take notice of information completeness. Profiles that have little or no work experience or education listed, or there are no endorsements or recommendations are signs of either a fake account or an inept networker (or possibly a brand new LinkedIn user).

Reviewing a connection request from a stranger by making these checks is quick, simple, and can filter legitimate connection requests from ones that offer little or no value.

Making Requests

Networking is a two-way street. Sometimes, you will be the one making a connection request of someone you do not know. Accept that some people will ignore your invitation because they do not know you. It is their policy for deciding how to act on connection invitations.

While you will not have a 100% success rate in connecting with people you do not know, take the following steps to increase the chances of making the connections you want:

- *Ask for introductions.* Your first-degree connections know people you do not but might benefit from meeting. Ask a first-degree connection to introduce a second-degree connection (i.e., a connection common to you and a first-degree connection). You can make this request by clicking the profile of the person to whom you want to be introduced. Click More beneath the person's profile headline (desktop platform). Select the option Share Profile and send as a message to the connection you would like to serve as introduction-maker. On the mobile platform, click three dots beside profile phot and select Share. Tell your connection why you want to connect with the other person and provide any other information that can be shared when making the introduction. Be sure to acknowledge the help given by the introduction-maker and be willing to pay it forward when you are the one asked to make an introduction.

- *Make it personal.* Never lose sight that LinkedIn is a *social* network—be sociable! You can make a positive first impression when reaching out to a stranger with a connection invitation by tailoring the invitation to introduce yourself. Be clear in stating why you want to connect and how you see a connection as being mutually beneficial.

- *Follow first.* If you feel inviting strangers to connect is too forward, take an intermediate step toward getting to know the person. You can first follow the person; it is a one-way relationship much like following someone on Twitter. When you follow a LinkedIn user, that person's activity will appear in your news feed. It is a way to get to know them better by reading their content and interacting with it by liking, sharing, or commenting. It also enables the person you follow to learn of and about you. To follow a user, click More underneath a user's profile headline and select Follow (desktop platform). If using LinkedIn's mobile platform, click the three dots to the right of the person's profile photo and select Follow.

Even if you are transparent with people you invite to connect, you will still face rejection. Do not take it personally; their view of what LinkedIn should do for them differs from yours.

Act on It

It is time to step out of your comfort zone by considering the benefits of connecting with people you do not know. Put yourself in situations of handling connection invitations from strangers and making them:

- The next connection invitation received from someone you do not know, follow the three actions in this chapter (read their profile, find out why they want to connect, and judge the potential benefit of adding the person to your network). Adopt the mindset that you are open to connections and will ignore invitations only if the requester cannot communicate the benefits to connect.

- Identify one person you do not know with whom you would like to connect on LinkedIn. Make a connection request directly, ask for an introduction from a shared connection, or follow the person with the intent of getting to know him or her.

15

Plays Well with Others

What are best practices for engagement?

For many years, LinkedIn seemed to be a social network in name only. It could be difficult to find much in the way of social interactions occurring there. In contrast, Facebook and Twitter did not have a cloud of awkwardness hovering over them. LinkedIn users were not as active in engaging with their connections as they were on other social networking sites.

Today, LinkedIn is a more active hub where people are being more sociable. You will realize value from LinkedIn only to the extent to which you are willing to engage with other users… but what does that mean, and how do you do it?

Defining Engagement

The terms "engagement" and "engage" come up frequently in marketing circles. Engagement is essential for building relationships, yet too often, we must assume what a call for engagement means. These takes on engagement offer guidance on what we should seek to accomplish:

- "Two-way communication"
- "The discovery and exchange of shared values and interests."

- "Connectedness, or creating a closer relationship with your audience."

First, engagement is about encouraging two-way communication. You can easily find content in the feeds of your social media accounts that is pretty much the opposite—chest thumping, I-am-great, even borderline narcissistic posts from people who are broadcasting, not communicating with others.

Second, engagement is about finding common ground with other people. We can learn and grow with the help of others when making ourselves available to ask, share, and discuss.

Third, the aim of engagement is to reach a higher state of connectedness with your network or audience. Content alone will not achieve that state; it is merely a starting point for the engagement journey.

Engagement Best Practices

Engaging with your connections and other LinkedIn users has similarities with other social networks as well as unique engagement opportunities. Make the following tactics regular practices in your LinkedIn usage:

- *Share updates.* It is OK for some content to be initiated by you, but it should not always be about you. As you post updates, ask yourself what potential value your connections and other LinkedIn users could receive from the update.

- *Publish articles.* Writing articles to post on LinkedIn Publishing not only allows you to articulate your point-of-view, but it also can serve as a conversation starter. People who read your posts may respond with comments or alternative viewpoints. The aim of an article should be to encourage dialogue on the topic. In fact, an article should include a call-to-action for readers, encouraging them to discuss.

- *Participate in Groups.* You can start or join in conversations with a targeted audience through Groups. Most groups are topic-specific, leading you to people who work in a particular industry or job, or they share similar interests with you. Participating in Groups offers opportunities to engage in many ways—like, comment, ask a question, provide answers, and even find new connections.

- *Send private messages.* It is not necessary for all engagement activity to be public. Using LinkedIn messaging feature, you can opt for one-on-one communication with connections. Messaging enables you to tailor engagement to an individual user or group of users. The same rule applies as for any form of content: There must be value for the recipient, not just you as the sender.

- *Offer congratulations.* Acknowledge milestones in connections' lives when you see them appear in your notifications—a birthday, new job, promotion, work anniversary, or award. These events are important to the people who achieve them. Give credit where credit is due and congratulate them.

- *Give thanks.* When someone shows you some love by taking time to endorse, recommend, share, comment, or like, take a moment to recognize his or her engagement with you.

- *Share others' ideas.* A guideline for how to engage through social media content is the 4-1-1 rule:
  - o 4 – Share four pieces of content created by others

- o 1 – Share one piece of content about you or your brand
- o 1 – Share one piece of content with a call-to-action component

The ratio does not have to be exactly 4-1-1, but the point of emphasis is clear: Content we share should be by others and for the benefit of others.

You may see a common thread in these practices: emphasizing the interests of others. Leadership expert John Maxwell said, "People don't care how much you know until they know how much you care." Engagement is a means to express caring.

Your LinkedIn communication should be others-focused. That is, how can your personal brand messaging be of value to others? Remember that people have limited time and attention resources. Your audience will appreciate efforts to engage them, in part because you will stand out from the noise that exists in the form of one-way communication.

Act on It

Do one of the engagement practices described in this chapter that is currently not part of your LinkedIn activity for the next week. Then, if there is another one that you do not practice regularly, focus on using it the next week. The goal is to expand the ways you engage with your network and others.

16

Social Proof

Do endorsements and recommendations matter?

A brand is an interesting entity. The brand owner controls many aspects of a brand. Observable attributes like name, appearance, and product features come to mind. These attributes hold meaning in the minds of people who encounter it. However, brand meaning ultimately resides in the minds and hearts of those people to whom a brand matters. If a brand is irrelevant to you, chances are you would not spend time assigning meaning to it.

For all of our efforts to manage perceptions about our personal brand, perceptions of others will largely shape our brand's image. This characteristic of personal branding is evident in the content of a LinkedIn profile. We create much of the content in our profile, but one section brings credibility to your brand through input given by others. The profile section Skills & Recommendations is where people viewing your profile can get a glimpse of how your brand is perceived by others.

When you are endorsed for a skill listed on your profile or someone writes a recommendation on your behalf, you are accumulating what is referred to as social proof. It is one thing for us to claim competence or strength with a skill or topic. However, a different reaction is elicited when people make claims of competence or strength about us. Positive feedback about your capabilities in the form of skill endorsements and recommendations affirms the brand identity projected in your profile portrays.

Validation of your personal brand through endorsements and recommendations can also serve as a signal to others unfamiliar with you how you offer unique value. In this situation, creating social proof is even more crucial as others infer about brand quality and reputation based on input your connections have given through endorsements and recommendations.

Some people hold the belief that their work should speak for itself. It is possible, but the impact of your work can be amplified when others endorse and recommend you. Similarly, you are able to acknowledge the value offered by people you know by endorsing or recommending them. The answer to the question "Do endorsements and recommendations matter?" should be a clear "yes."

Endorsements and recommendations were introduced in chapter 7 as part of building your profile. Now, we examine these elements of your LinkedIn profile further to consider the best ways to receive and give feedback through endorsements and recommendations.

Skills Endorsements

You can list up to 50 skills in your profile, although a more compact skills list emphasizes greatest strengths and reduces noise in your profile. A list of 15 skills will be easier for your connections to scan and react to than a list of 45 skills.

One way skills are validated occurs when connections endorse you for skills in your profile. Endorsements are less specific and detailed than recommendations. Thus, they are generally perceived as having less weight or influence than recommendations. Think of endorsements as a virtual thumbs-up about a person's skills.

One reason endorsements are perceived to have less impact than recommendations is they require little more effort than clicking on a skill listed under the Skills & Endorsements section on a user's profile. The ease of endorsing others inadvertently creates a drawback to endorsements. The norm of reciprocity potentially reduces giving and receiving endorsements to a game of "you scratch my back, and I'll scratch yours."

Endorsements do not carry the same weight as recommendations due to the absence of supporting evidence. Clicking to endorse someone could be a gut feeling that the person has that skill, not rooted in evidence he or she has demonstrated the skill. In contrast, a recommendation is more descriptive, like a user review for a product. Making an endorsement can be done in three easy steps:

1. Visit a first-degree connection's profile
2. Find the section "Featured Skills & Endorsements"
3. Click on skills for which you want to endorse the connection.

Could you ask others to endorse you for specific skills? Yes, but the most effective way to entice connections to endorse you is give them a reason to take action. That reason could be as simple as endorsing them for skills you perceive as their strengths. The norm of reciprocity often takes over, and you will have endorsements from that person soon thereafter. In general, if you consistently offer value to other people, it is more likely to be recognized. Skill endorsements are a small token of acknowledgement for one's good work.

Despite the limitations of endorsements, they still are a valuable source of social proof. Receiving endorsements is not only beneficial to your profile, but endorsing connections' strengths is good networking practice. You are recognizing their value.

Recommendations

In contrast to endorsements, recommendations are detailed summaries of a LinkedIn user's strengths or capabilities. The content of a recommendation is similar to that found in a letter of recommendation you might ask someone to write on your behalf when applying for a job or graduate school. The maximum length for a recommendation is 3,000 characters (roughly 500 words). Thus, someone writing a recommendation can give summary impressions of you as well as share details and examples about your strengths or skills.

Recommendations are effective for offering social proof about your brand's value. While recommendations can be invaluable for someone actively seeking a job, you need not be on the job market to utilize recommendations in your profile. Adopt these practices for making recommendations a tool that works for you:

- *Seek recommendations when you do not need them.* A sign that someone is undergoing job transition is a sudden increase in LinkedIn activity. When I get a connection or recommendation requests from former students, it is common to find in their profile that they are between jobs. Finding yourself unemployed can be a shock, but you can take steps to minimize the impact of the situation by having your personal brand brochure (i.e., your LinkedIn profile) current and fully developed.

In short, ask for and make recommendations periodically regardless of your employment status. Business expert and author Harvey Mackay described this mindset as "dig your well before you're thirsty."

- *Be selective.* Only request recommendations from first-degree connections who know you well. It can be awkward for a person to write a recommendation for someone with whom they have little familiarity with their strengths and capabilities. The quality of an endorsement correlates with how well the writer knows the endorsee. Overall, fewer high quality endorsements carry more weight than a high quantity of endorsements containing little substance.

- *Make it personal.* Any request of a LinkedIn user should be personalized. Let the other person know why you have reached out for his or her endorsement and how it would benefit you. LinkedIn allows a requester to tailor a recommendation request by selecting options that tells the person receiving the request in what role you have been associated and what organizations you share a connection. Personalizing the recommendation request also helps the person asked to write it as you can suggest points to include. The writer will likely appreciate input you give on what to include or what you seek to accomplish.

  Follow the practice of personalizing recommendation requests even if you know the person well. An impersonal recommendation request comes across as laziness on the requester's part. Don't be lazy!

So, how do you write or request recommendations? Visit a connection's profile and do the following to write a recommendation:

1. Go to profile of a first-degree connection
2. Click the box "More" under their profile headline
3. Select "Recommend"

To request a recommendation:

1. Go to profile of a first-degree connection
2. Click the box "More" under their profile headline
3. Select "Request a Recommendation"

Act on It

Endorsements and recommendations are two-way streets. While the suggestions in this chapter are primarily about receiving these forms of social proof, you must commit to being on the giving end, too. Give-to-get is not just a cute expression, it is human nature. Make endorsements and recommendations part of your networking activity.

- Commit to making skills endorsements for one first-degree connection each time you are on LinkedIn. Your connections offer value; let others know about their value by endorsing skills you have observed.

- Write a recommendation for someone who has served or helped you. Many of us would give unsolicited feedback about a product or employee that exceeded expectations. Why not show similar love for someone you know?

17

Groupthink

What role should Groups play in my LinkedIn experience?

Finding and meeting people with similar interests is one of the most rewarding benefits of social media. We can connect with people around the world with no more than a few keyboard strokes and mouse clicks. LinkedIn is no exception to connecting with others. In addition to networking with other users one-on-one, LinkedIn's Groups feature provides gathering places for users around a shared interest—an industry, topic, geographic location, alma mater, or company, to name a few.

If you subscribe to the definition of networking as "building good relationships," LinkedIn Groups is a channel that fosters doing just that.

Understanding Groups

Groups are user-driven networking vehicles. LinkedIn users form, manage, and moderate groups. A user can form a group to encourage people to gather around a topic or shared interest. Groups privacy settings options are standard or unlisted. Standard groups will appear in search results, while unlisted groups do not. Joining an unlisted group requires an invitation sent by a group manager. Even with standard groups, you will often have to request to join the group. It is the group owner's attempt to maintain quality and minimize aggressive selling tactics by group members more interested in promoting their products or themselves.

You may join up to 100 groups on LinkedIn. Two schools of thought exist regarding the number of groups to join. One school of thought is join as many groups as you want since you can belong to up to 100 of them. Doing so allows you to explore various interests and potentially network with a wider audience.

The other school of thought is to be selective in which groups you join. It is harder to have quality interactions with group members when you belong to a large number of groups. Focus on a small number of groups and be active in them by starting discussions, commenting and liking others' posts, and getting to know fellow group members.

Each side has valid points on whether to take a narrow or broad approach to Groups membership. You will have to find the optimal number of groups for you based on how varied your interests are. Also, consider the amount of time you can devote to networking on LinkedIn. In short, more time spent on LinkedIn could support more group memberships.

So what happens in groups? If you have used LinkedIn for some time, you will notice group pages have been redesigned to more resemble the user experience in the news feed. Group members will ask a question, post an article, or share some other content to start group discussion. Benefits of engaging in conversations include learning from fellow group members, helping others solve problems, and receiving exposure to diverse thought. Group members can post job opportunities in the Jobs section, giving users another outlet to search for job opportunities on LinkedIn.

Finding Groups

You may have little experience with the Groups feature even if you are a long-time LinkedIn user. The idea of joining groups may be appealing, but you are unsure how to find the right groups for you. Become more comfortable navigating Groups by using these tactics:

- To find groups, type in a search term (topic, industry, geographic location, company, or institution). Groups is one of the filtering options for which you can choose to view results. Then, review search results by clicking on groups that are interesting and learn more in the About This Group section on the group's page.

- If you are new to Groups, one way to get ideas for groups to join is to look at group memberships of some of your first-degree connections. You can see their groups in their profile under Interests.

- Find groups to join by checking out profiles of second-degree connections under People You May Know. These users likely have something in common with you, including interests in the form of groups to which they belong. Joining some of the same groups as your second-degree connections gives you even more common ground. This step can help if you wish to connect with them eventually.

Act on It

Groups are an under-utilized tool on LinkedIn. Most users do not take the time to enter into conversations or network with group members regardless of their number of group memberships. Groups need not be a missed opportunity for you. Complement one-on-one interactions with your connections through group memberships.

Review how Groups adds to your experience by doing the following:

- If you belong to groups, review each one to see how much activity (i.e., conversations) there have been recently. Is it an active group in terms of number of conversations and engagement with conversations? Leave groups that are not active or are no longer valuable to you.

- Look for new groups to join by using the search feature. Review results and read more about groups that intrigue you. Also, review the profile of five first-degree connections with whom you have common interests. Are there groups to which they belong but you do not? If so, check out some of their groups, and if you find them interesting, join them.

- Each time you are on LinkedIn, commit to visiting one of the group pages to which you belong. Doing so will enable you to be familiar with topics being discussed as well as the group members active in conversations.

18

Your Networking Pulse

How can content benefit my networking activity?

In addition to being a place for professionals to connect and network, LinkedIn offers a platform for sharing ideas and opinions. LinkedIn acquired Pulse, a content aggregation app, in 2013. Over time, LinkedIn integrated the Pulse platform user experience to the point it is no longer a standalone product. Today, you can find articles published by LinkedIn users using the search function. Content is one of the categories of search results displayed.

What does reading articles have to do with growing your network? It is a passive activity compared to interacting with other people, but do not underestimate the value of discovering new connections by searching and reading content. Learning is not the only outcome coming from reading articles. Some of the authors and fellow readers of articles published on LinkedIn could very well be future connections.

Why LinkedIn Articles?

Becoming a consumer of LinkedIn articles is beneficial in two important ways. First, reading articles written by other LinkedIn users exposes you to diverse thought and opinion. It pushes you beyond an echo chamber to consider other viewpoints. While you likely will find authors whose latest articles you eagerly await to read, other authors unknown to you have valuable insights from which you can learn.

Second, interacting with article authors, whether they are connections or strangers, is an easy way to engage others. If you feel stuck in terms of what to say or do on LinkedIn, liking, commenting, and sharing what others have written put you on their radar. They will appreciate the acknowledgement of their articles, too.

From Reading to Networking

Reading articles can contribute to self-development, but you are missing a golden networking opportunity if you do not engage authors and readers. People who write articles and the readers commenting, sharing, or liking them are signaling interest in a topic. If you share that interest, these people are prospects with whom to make a connection and build relationships.

Article authors on LinkedIn might be influencers you do not know. However, you may find that an author with whom you want to connect is a second-degree connection (i.e., a connection of one of your connections). Ask the mutual connection to make an introduction. Be sure to explain to the mutual connection why you would like to be introduced.

Remember that requesting a connection is not the only way to interact with others on LinkedIn. Follow authors whose content you find interesting, even if you do not know them. Doing so can be a first step toward making a connection with that person. It is more of a slow build than being introduced by a mutual connection or a cold-call connection request (which is not advisable).

Articles can find their way into your feed because connections or users you follow published them. Extend the reach of articles (and the people with whom you could network) by using hashtags. LinkedIn makes it easier for users to filter content by relevant hashtags. Search hashtags to find people who post content on topics of interest to you. Some of these people you may know or have heard of them; others will be new to you.

Finding people using a hashtag search exposes you to content that you may not see otherwise. Moreover, it can introduce you to potential new connections. For example, I did a hashtag search for #sponsorship (a long-time academic research interest of mine). Of the first ten users in the search results who had written articles or made posts using #sponsorship, nine of them were people I did not know nor had a connection with in any way. The search introduced me to people from whom I can learn and even establish relationships.

Act on It

Articles published on LinkedIn offer dual benefits of learning and networking. Take advantage of these two impacts on personal growth by trying these tactics:

- Read five articles appearing in your feed. Be sure to read comments if any appear after the article. Take note of the author and commenter(s). If you are not connected to the person, visit their profile to determine if you have second-degree (i.e., mutual) connections. If yes, ask the second-degree connection to make an introduction. If no, follow the user in order to receive updates on their activity in your feed. Set the stage for networking with them after becoming better acquainted with them through their content.

- Do three hashtag searches on topics or keywords of interest to you. Then, repeat the previous tactic and read articles in the search results with the relevant hashtag. Identify people with whom you would like to connect and utilize second-degree connections to make an introduction or follow them. Take action to turn these strangers into connections.

19

Mentor Wanted

Can I use LinkedIn to find a mentor?

Someone gave you the advice "you need a mentor." Perhaps the thought of having a mentor crossed your mind. You long to have a mentor offer guidance because of lack of direction or success. Regardless of how you come to seeking a mentor, the trajectory of your professional development could depend on whether you have a mentor in your corner.

The word mentor is both a noun and verb. Mentor as a noun refers to an experienced and trusted adviser. The verb mentor is the act of advising or training. Bottom line: You can benefit from a mentor who mentors you.

If you believe a mentor would not be valuable for your development, you are in the minority. An estimated 80% of LinkedIn users are open to being involved with mentoring, either as a mentor (teacher) or mentee (pupil). The significant interest in mentoring among LinkedIn users suggests it is fertile ground to find a mentor (or offer your guidance as a mentor).

First Things First

Yes, this chapter is about how to find a mentor on LinkedIn. Before we go down that path, let's take a step back and consider exactly who a mentor is and what he or she does. What are characteristics of an effective mentor? Someone with knowledge, experience, and a deep network are desirable points on a checklist, but those qualities alone do not mean a mentor will be good for you.

A mentor's experience does little good if their availability is inconsistent. They must be open to giving their time to mentor you, whether it be by email, phone conversations, text messaging, or face-to-face meetings.

An effective mentor strikes a balance between being a cheerleader and drill sergeant. While you want a mentor to be supportive, they should challenge you, too. Constructive criticism and encouraging a mentee to leave his or her comfort zone are qualities of a mentor that contribute to the mentee's growth.

Ideally, you and a mentor will have similar values and goals. This shared vision can be difficult to discern when you first meet someone. However, you can observe clues about a person through his or her posts, articles, and comments. Do your homework to determine if someone you would like to approach as a mentor is on the same page as you when it comes to values, beliefs, and outlook.

Doing Your Homework

Different interaction points with LinkedIn users can be places where you discover a prospective mentor. These interaction points include:

o *First-degree connections.* You know them, and they know you. The search for a mentor may require little searching.

o *Second-degree connections.* Persons with whom you have mutual connections, but you are not connected with each other. An introduction by a mutual connection can get the relationship off on the right foot.

o *LinkedIn article authors.* Chapter 18 covered using articles as a networking tool. Go a step further and evaluate authors as possible mentors.

o *LinkedIn Groups.* You have something in common with everyone who belongs to the same group(s) as you. This characteristic may seem trivial, but it is a signal that you have shared interests.

o *People you encounter in real life.* Have you ever been impressed by someone you met at a conference, party, or other social setting? Maybe you see him or her as the type of person with whom you would enjoy spending time. Although we are talking about finding a mentor and not drinking buddies, enjoying the company of someone who can teach and coach you is a plus.

Regardless of where you locate prospective mentor (or mentors as it is OK to have more than one), take it slow. Begin by following the person rather than requesting a connection (assuming you have not had prior interactions). Take a give-to-get approach, offering value to the person through likes, shares, or comments. Doing so can bring awareness about you to the person. After connecting with the person, continue to add value by sharing posts or articles you think would be of interest. The stage is now set to ask for more: a one-to-one interaction that deepens the relationship.

If the suggestions for identifying a mentor seem too cumbersome, one more option exists. LinkedIn facilitates forming mentor-mentee connections through the Career Advice feature. Users can use Career Advice to indicate if they are seeking advice or willing to give advice.

To access the Career Advice hub on desktop, click "Me" then select "View Profile." Then, scroll down to Your Dashboard and select the Career Advice hub.

In the Career Advice hub, you can edit preferences on expertise and industry affiliation of persons from whom you would like to receive advice. Then, add a message in your own words about what you would like to know or receive in terms of information or guidance. You will get a recommended list of LinkedIn users who are willing to give advice. Message person(s) to initiate a conversation. It could be the beginning of a mentor-mentee relationship.

Act on It

Approaching someone about a mentoring relationship can be intimidating. Fortunately, LinkedIn offers a channel in which people are likely to be open to being a mentor. If you are in search of a mentor, take the following steps to find a possible match:

- Review the five interaction points shared in the Doing Your Homework section. Identify at least one person from each of the five interaction points. Next, rank these five people on their suitability as a mentor. Remember to take it slow, but begin laying the foundation for a relationship with the person you ranked number one as a prospective mentor. Go down the list and work on establishing a relationship with the others.

- Use LinkedIn's Career Advice hub to seek advice as the first step toward finding a mentor. It is possible that the feedback you receive from someone sends a signal that you would not want that person to be your mentor... and that is OK. You will not find a mentor unless you put yourself out there as someone who is willing to be mentored.

Part III: Creating

20

Publish or Perish

What is an effective LinkedIn content strategy?

Yeah, the chapter title might be a bit too provocative. You will have to forgive me because in my position as an academic, job security and career advancement depend on the ability to publish content. When it comes to your personal brand, publish or perish has implications, too. While job termination may not happen because you did not publish enough content, lack of a presence created by content publication could hinder your potential to advance. Content enhances your visibility among your peers, bosses, and clients.

Social media in general and LinkedIn in particular give you a platform for publishing content. A well-kept secret may be good when talking about a great restaurant you discovered. Being a relative unknown within your organization or industry is a different matter. Don't be a well-kept secret!

LinkedIn's Content Capabilities

Content is a source of value you have to offer current and potential connections on LinkedIn. Of course, LinkedIn is used for purposes other than content distribution and consumption, namely networking. Content is essential for realizing one of the prime benefits of using LinkedIn: learning. As you begin thinking about developing a content strategy for LinkedIn, consider the content forms and types available.

Two general content forms include posts and articles. A post, also called a status update, is content that appears in the news feed of other users. An article is longer, blog-like content published using LinkedIn's native author platform. Within posts, various content types include:

- Text posts (can include external links to other pages)
- Photos
- Documents
- Video
- Slides
- Original articles

Consider your strengths when deciding which content type(s) to incorporate into your content strategy. For example, if you enjoy creating visual messages like photos and slides, look for opportunities to use visual media in your posts. You are not limited to a single content type.

Content creation is one consideration for your content strategy; content distribution is another one. You can control distribution of posts if you wish to manage who sees your posts. For each post made, distribution settings from which to choose include:

- Public (all LinkedIn users)
- Public + Twitter (if you have your Twitter account linked)
- Connections (your first-degree connections)

In addition, you can control engagement for any post, deciding whether to allow comments (default) or disable comments.

Your Content Strategy

Many brands are influential in the marketplace because they strategically use communication to build awareness and reinforce their value. Similarly, you can use communication to establish your personal brand's value. LinkedIn is an ideal channel for many professionals to reach their target market. Being there is a start, but develop a strategy for using content. The process for a LinkedIn content marketing strategy includes the following four steps.

1. *Set a goal for content publishing.* What should your content accomplish? Some possible goals include:

   - Establishing visibility for your personal brand
   - Positioning yourself as a thought leader
   - Being a resource to others in your field
   - Creating a lead generation tool to find new clients

2. *Decide on mix of content forms and types.* Pick the media that will be the focus of your content publishing (status updates, articles, links to articles, infographics, etc.).

3. *Set frequency goals for different content types.* Commit to a consistent presence for your brand. A simple example:

   - Two status updates daily
   - Three article shares per week
   - Three other shares per week (e.g., video, document, slides)
   - One original article every two weeks

4. *Review activity and engagement with your content.* A final, critical step in content marketing is evaluating performance. Review content published on LinkedIn regularly to measure the following outcomes:

- Number of likes, shares, and comments triggered by each type of content.

- Content types with low engagement, quality and frequency of content posted. Experiment with different content, frequency, or day/time posted in an effort to improve effectiveness.

- New connections occurring from content published. Which content types are bringing new connections or followers? What topics or subjects are attracting people to your network?

Content strategy is not an option. You will not get the most out of LinkedIn if you do not have a plan for using content to amplify your personal brand.

Act on It

Publishing content on LinkedIn is one of the greatest contributions you can make to your network. Posts and articles that inform, educate, or inspire add value to other users. Content effectiveness over the long run depends on having a strategy so that your content has a purpose. Otherwise, it contributes to the noise on social media.

Implement the four steps of the content marketing strategy process. To do this, go through these steps:

1. Set at least one goal for publishing content.
2. Decide on the mix of content forms and types to publish. Strive for variety in your content, but leverage the forms you are most comfortable creating.
3. Set frequency goals for each content type you will use.
4. Review performance of your content. How is each form (posts or articles) and type performing in terms of likes, views, shares, and comments?

21

Avoid Writer's Block

How do I come up with ideas for writing LinkedIn articles?

LinkedIn's publishing platform gives you a voice, not to mention an audience of more than 500 million users. You may be sold on the benefits of publishing articles—building brand awareness, positioning as a thought leader, and expanding your network—to name three. One not-so-minor detail remains: What should you write about that other users would find interesting and valuable?

Understand that you need to commit to an ongoing article generation program for your brand. LinkedIn expert Mark Williams recommends publishing at least one or two articles a month. However, coming up with processes for ideation and writing articles could be overwhelming.

To tackle the challenge of creating original articles, break it down into two steps: 1) deciding what topics to write about and 2) coming up with writing strategies.

What to Write?

Appreciating the benefits of writing articles is one thing; having a system for generating article ideas can be more challenging to establish. Uncertainties about what to write can be enough to stymie a plan for publishing LinkedIn articles before getting it off the ground.

Overcome writer's block before it sets in by trying the following system to find topics for your LinkedIn articles:

- *What topics interest you?* Start by pinpointing topics that spark interest. Keep in mind you do not have to be an expert. Topics that pique curiosity or prompt deeper thinking are ideal starting points.

- *What topics are others writing about on LinkedIn?* Your news feed can reveal what matters to your potential audience. The next three points delve into this question.

   - Spend 5-10 minutes a day in your news feed, looking for posts and articles with five or more comments. What are the posts and articles about?

   - Note the authors of posts or articles with five or more comments. View their profile and check out other posts and articles they have written. On what topics are they writing? Review their posts and articles to determine how many likes, comments, and shares they received. These numbers are indicators of topic popularity.

   - Search topics using hashtags related to topics that interest you. Review search results to identify content with five or more comments just as you did in your news feed. Review authors' posts for insight into topics about which they are writing.

Think of these steps like mining for precious minerals. You are digging into your news feed and authors' profiles,

not knowing exactly what you will find. Some digs will turn up little useful results; other digs will be rich in ideas for writing LinkedIn articles.[1]

Compelling Content

Once you have a topic in mind about which you will write, you may still be struggling with the form your idea should take. The good news is many options exist for creating content that will attract readers. Different approaches to writing an article include:

- Implications of a current event
- Trends affecting your industry
- Predictions about trends that stand to impact your industry
- Challenges you have faced
- Opportunities you have seized
- Lessons learned through experience
- Advice for someone starting in your field

These approaches reflect a range of how much you wish to reveal about yourself. Writing on a current event, discussing trends, or making predictions are conservative ways to express your viewpoint. The content you create reacts to what is going on around you.

In contrast, the other four approaches are more personal and can reveal vulnerabilities or failures. Allowing others to see the real you can attract an audience if others perceive similarity with you.

---

[1] For a detailed description on a process for coming up with ideas for articles, listen to an episode of the LinkedInformed podcast on this subject (http://linkedinformed.com/episode162/).

Act on It

You cannot afford to wait on perfecting a content creation process before implementing it. Author Margaret Atwood, who has written more than 40 books, said, "If I waited for perfection, I would never write a word." Don't wait! Try the actions described earlier in this chapter for ideation:

- Spend 5-10 minutes a day reviewing your news feed for posts and articles with five or more comments. Make note of the topic.

- View the profile of the authors of these posts and articles, looking at other content they created to see what other activity generated five or more comments. Make note of the topic.

- Do hashtag searches in LinkedIn search to find content published on topics that interest you.

- Write! Publish an article this week. If you are struggling with how to put ideas into article format, use one of the seven approaches for writing an article given in this chapter (current event synopsis, predictions, challenges faced, etc.).

22

Anatomy of an Article

What are best practices for writing LinkedIn articles?

You have a strategy in place for content creation and publication. The plan is in place; you know what must happen next. It is time to write. I know how it feels to stare at the screen, not knowing what to write. You realize writing articles can have a positive impact on your brand, but that realization does little to transfer words from brain to screen.

If you have not been frightened away yet, we will tackle constructing a LinkedIn article. Once you get a feel for article layout and find a voice with which you are comfortable, you will eliminate the avoidance strategy under which you have operated.

What to Include

Even if you are new to LinkedIn articles, you likely are familiar with the structure a typical article. Why? LinkedIn articles have structure and appearance that resemble blog posts. They have a structure and look common to blog posts you read online. As you compose articles to publish on LinkedIn, examine the following elements to determine if you are employing best practices.

Headline
1. How-to and "listicle" (list-style article) headlines generate more page views than question headlines.
2. One recommendation for headline length is 40-50 characters.

Visuals
3. Use a header image to draw attention to article.
4. In addition, use images within the article (e.g., photo, graphs, charts, and drawings).
5. Only use images for which you have permission. Do not appropriate the creative work of others. Many sources exist for royalty-free stock photo images if you need them such as Pixabay, Flickr, and Unsplash.
6. Give credit for images to their creator or owner, even ones for which you have permission.

Formatting
7. Use headings and subheadings to break down long passages into shorter, easy to read blocks.
8. Link to relevant sources mentioned in your article. For example, if you mention a book, include a link to the author's website or the book's page on Amazon. Adding links to articles gives readers value beyond your thoughts and viewpoint.
9. If you have a website, link to the homepage or a relevant page on the site. Use LinkedIn's massive reach to drive people to your website who would otherwise not come across it.

10. Include a call-to-action, even if it is nothing more than inviting comments or other feedback on an article's topic.

Presentation

The ten points presented in the preceding section summarize style elements often found in well-written LinkedIn articles. However, structure is not enough. In fact, following checklists like this one as the sole guide for writing an article can lead to a me-too situation. If we all apply the same lists, we run the risk of our content looking the same, thus lacking a unique style or voice.

Adopting best practices and adhering to a certain structure is helpful for writing articles. However, you must complement those approaches with an emphasis on speaking in a voice that feels natural to you.

Consider the following practices when determining your presentation style:

- *Longer articles are more likely to be shared.* More than two-thirds of articles are less than 1,000 words, but articles between 1,000-3,000 words are shared more often than shorter ones. If getting shares is important (e.g., for adding new connections or finding sales leads), longer pieces are more likely to achieve that result.

- *Write in a voice consistent with your personality.* Fortunately, message effectiveness is not limited to one voice type. Be yourself, and your style with resonate with some people. It will not resonate with everyone, but since not everyone wants what you have to sell (and yes, you are selling yourself, if nothing else) you do not have to worry about appealing to everyone. In my case, my experience as a teacher influences me to write in a style that is similar to teaching in the classroom. If you are a gifted storyteller, use that gift to present your idea and message.

- *Certain phrases pique interest of readers.* Research into characteristics of the most shared articles on LinkedIn by marketing services company BuzzSumo found the following phrases occurring with highest frequency:
    - How to
    - Ways to
    - The best
    - At work
    - You should

The common thread in these keywords is they respond to readers' desire to gain something from reading an article—knowledge, skill enhancement, or something that gives them an edge.

Act on It

The time to write your next (or first) LinkedIn article is now, not tomorrow, next week, or next month. You have something to offer; do not keep it from us any longer!

Take action by writing a LinkedIn article. Before pressing the Publish button, review your article using the 10-point checklist in this chapter. Revise elements as needed and publish.

23

Lights, Camera, Action!

Should I use video to publish content?

The iconic cable television network Music Television (MTV) debuted on August 1, 1981. The first video played featured a British new wave band, The Buggles. The video for the song "Video Killed the Radio Star" foretold the impact video would have on the music industry. It was not long before new artists adept at video creation built a following. Established artists who embraced video as a new creative platform solidified their standing as marquee acts.

Fast forward to now, and we are witnessing a repeat of video's impact, this time in social media. Networks like Snapchat built an audience largely around video. Facebook, Twitter, and Instagram have tweaked their user experience to accommodate and encourage video. Then, there is LinkedIn.

Native video, or video content published directly to a website versus appearing via a link from another website, was not a feature offered by LinkedIn until 2017. While LinkedIn lagged behind other social networking sites, the good news is video has arrived. Video is an important communication channel for expanding your audience and delivering value in new ways.

Why Video?

If you are skeptical about using video on LinkedIn, or you think you have a face to be a writer (and not be on camera), consider how video offsets some limitations imposed by text-dominant communication. First realize that text-based communications present limitations. Online communication in particular is cluttered with predominantly text posts. The clutter created by the large volume of text content means your words many not only be ignored, but worse, never seen. While words are powerful they cannot match the creative impact of visual content. Video does not force the message sender to choose between words and pictures. Video enables you to utilize words and imagery to inform, entertain, or persuade.

Second, regardless of whether you are comfortable being in front of a camera, content consumption via video has exploded. Video may be an emerging communication channel on LinkedIn, but it is entrenched as a means of reaching an audience. Statistics compiled by Insivia, an Internet marketing consulting firm, reveal video already has significant influence:

- 55% of people watch videos online every day.
- Four times as many customers would rather watch a video about a product than read about it.
- People spend 2.6 times longer on pages with video than pages without video.
- 500 million people watch videos on Facebook every day.
- Snapchat users watch a combined 10 billion videos a day.

Audiences are consuming video if it is available. Are you willing to do your part to satisfy the appetite for video content?

Video Execution

Before taking the plunge to go on-screen with native video, be aware of the parameters for video content on LinkedIn. Video length must be between three seconds and ten minutes, with file size not exceeding five gigabytes. While compelling content of any length will likely attract viewers, strive to make videos on the lower end of the time spectrum.

The use of video on LinkedIn is too new to have insight into optimal length. However, research into video length on YouTube has found the videos are on average about 4 minutes, 20 seconds. That said, expect to lose viewers the longer a video is. Video marketing agency Wistia found that 75% of viewers watch a video of 1-2 minutes long, but the videos 4-5 minutes long retain fewer than 60% of viewers to the end. In other words, brevity matters.

It is not required that you invest in expensive equipment to get into the video game on LinkedIn. The camera on your smartphone or a webcam can do the job. Of course, it is possible to enhance the quality of video posts by selecting camera, microphone, backdrop, and editing software that deliver the desired finished product.

Posting native video can be done on the desktop or mobile platform. To upload video on LinkedIn's desktop platform, click Video in the same box you go to when posting text or images. Upload the desired video file when prompted. LinkedIn's mobile app lets you record video on the spot and upload to your feed. Click to share an article photo, video, or idea just under the search bar. Then, click the video icon and it's lights, camera, action!

Act on It

LinkedIn is a relative newcomer to offering native video as a communication channel, so many users are still figuring out how to use video to their advantage. You have an opportunity to create a distinctive niche through video content.

You probably have guessed the action item for this chapter: make a video post to LinkedIn! Experiment with posting native video by creating a message around one of the following topics:

- Your take on a news story or current trend affecting your industry.

- Advice or other insight to young people (students and early career professionals) from your experiences.

- Acknowledgement of service or benefit received from someone in your network or a company with whom you do business.

Part IV: Seeking

24

Seek and You Shall Find

What are ways to use LinkedIn as a job search resource?

If you give credence to statistics, chances are you will be looking for a job at some point in your working years. An estimated three million American workers quit their job each month. That figure does not count layoffs, terminations, or other involuntary separations. Many people are waiting for the day they can walk away. The obstacle is navigating the job search process to find a new opportunity.

You will probably not be surprised if I tell you LinkedIn can be a primary channel for direct and indirect job search. Direct job search can be measured in the number of jobs posted on LinkedIn, which one estimate put at 10 million per month. LinkedIn is invaluable for indirectly conducting a job search. Your connections know about openings not posted on LinkedIn. In addition, they may know the right people in organizations. They can connect you with leads and hiring managers that could ultimately result in you landing a new job.

Update Your Brochure

Advice on using LinkedIn to aid in job search will read more like a review of best practices covered throughout this book. It stands to reason as your personal branding efforts should keep your LinkedIn presentation fresh and up-to-date.

The suggested practices that follow should be familiar; they have come up already as ways to manage your brand presence on LinkedIn. If you find yourself in job search mode, revisit these action items to ensure your profile communicates value offered.

- Ensure your profile is complete and current.
- Consider whether your profile communicates your relevance to particular job or industry, tailoring it to be of interest to people and companies in your target industry.
- Make sure you have a customized URL for your LinkedIn profile to make it easier for people to find you.
- Add keywords to your profile that reflect your greatest strengths or skills.
- Streamline the experience section of your profile, removing outdated or irrelevant information.
- Update the skills section of your profile so that it reflects your current competencies.

Activate Job Search

Proactive management of your profile helps LinkedIn users find you and get a feel for your personal brand. However, making yourself easier to find and understand is not the only way to leverage your LinkedIn presence during a job search. In addition to marketing through your profile, implement these actions to make yourself more visible on LinkedIn.

- *Follow companies that interest you.* Keep up with news and people at companies that you consider dream employers. Staying informed about developments in these organizations can position you to pursue an opportunity. Many companies post job openings on their LinkedIn pages.

- *Join groups related to jobs or industries with which you aspire to identify* (revisit chapter 17 for more on groups). Interacting with group members can add to your network, make you more informed, and open the door to new relationships that could lead to landing a job.

- *Participate in groups.* Weighing in on topics can demonstrate your skills and knowledge when you start a discussion or contribute to other group members' discussions.

- *Publish articles on topics, trends, or current events impacting your chosen field.* Article authorship enables you to show a unique perspective that you can bring to an employer.

- *Use job search capabilities.* Search for jobs on LinkedIn under the Jobs tab in search results. Use jobs filters to refine your search and to search by date posted, experience level, specific location, job function, company, and industry. You can save job searches, and even receive emails about new job listings. You can also find job openings by searching for and clicking on specific companies.

One final piece of advice: Implement the practices that can help you land a job *before* you are looking for a job. With the exception of conducting job searches, all other recommended practices should be part of your ongoing LinkedIn activity. If you take this approach, the job search will be far easier to handle if and when you find yourself on the market.

Act on It

This chapter reinforces the advice "dig your well before you are thirsty." The time to swing into a job search mindset is not the day you are laid off or turn in your two-week notice. Following the practices reiterated in this chapter will serve you well on an ongoing basis.

If you are searching for a job, use LinkedIn's job search capabilities. In particular, make use of jobs filters options to narrow your search to find relevant, interesting opportunities. Now go search!

25

Put the Work in Network

How can networking on LinkedIn aid my job search?

Your professional network is one of the most valuable assets you can build over the course of a career. The network you cultivate can enrich you in several ways—as a source for learning, the origin of friendships, and, yes, connection point for new career opportunities, to name three.

While building a network holds these potential benefits, think of them as by-products of creating meaningful relationships. Ideally, networking is not used as a means to an end such as getting a new job. The broader goal should be to use networking (and LinkedIn) to build a distinctive personal brand.

When you create a trusted, reputable brand, opportunities such as new jobs will find you. That said, you could find yourself unexpectedly on the job market at some point in your career. Corporate downsizing, consolidation after a merger, or being on the wrong side of a bad boss could land you in the position of looking for new opportunity.

Whether you are forced into a job search or go there willingly, tap your network of connections on LinkedIn to advocate on your behalf.

Do the Work

Much of the work involved with using LinkedIn as a job search tool has nothing to do with jobs. If you embrace a mindset of "dig your well before you are thirsty," networking on LinkedIn is not something you are doing to land a job. Instead, you are doing it because you realize the benefits of building a strong network.

Two actions are crucial in turning your network into an indispensable asset. You have heard them before, so if you were hoping to get a recipe for a secret sauce for better networking you might be disappointed.

- *Build connections on an ongoing basis.* This suggestion is living the dig-your-well-before-you-are-thirsty mindset. Do not wait until you need connections to pursue them! Have them before you need them. I can predict with amazing accuracy when a former student is on the job market. The evidence adds up—a LinkedIn connection request out of the blue, a basic profile summary, and a handful of connections. This person has likely had an "oh no" event occur, as in "oh no, I am out of a job and unsure what to do now."
  Odds of experiencing an "oh no" moment decrease if you commit to raising the quality and quantity of connections. This commitment includes making new connections as well as keeping in touch with existing ones.

- *Give endorsements and recommendations.* This chapter is about how to help *you*. So, why talk about helping others? We return to another mindset that we should be practicing: give to get. The norm of reciprocity applies. Your connections are more likely to help you as a form of payback for you giving an endorsement or recommendation.

Note that we are not reducing this practice to a game. You may give and not get… and that is OK. But, if you never give endorsements or recommendations to others, should you realistically expect anyone to go to bat for you?

Reach Out to People You Know (And Don't Know)

The networking definition "building good relationships" suggests placing a premium on quality of connections. There are two types of people on LinkedIn: People you know and people you do not know. You can network with both types as you pursue a job opportunity. However, you must take different communication approaches with each type.

When networking with people you know, it may not be possible to inform them you are looking for a job (e.g., changing your headline to reflect you are searching). Use targeted messages to trusted connections, letting them know you are seeking a new opportunity. Ask for their assistance in passing along information on jobs for which you might be a fit. Connections can provide a valuable service by sharing your profile and making introductions to their connections that could help in your search.

Networking with people you do not know is riskier and takes patience. Some people with whom you would like to connect could be connections of people in your network (i.e., second-degree connections). In this situation, ask the mutual connection to share your profile with the person with whom you want to connect.

If you do not have a mutual connection but want to connect with the person, put these steps into action:

- *Follow first.* A user with whom you want to connect could be your next boss or colleague... if only you knew that person. The good news is you can take steps to make a connection request to that person. Begin by following the person. View the person's profile. Click More and select the Follow option. Unlike a connection request, following a user does not require reciprocation on their part. You will see their activity in your feed.

- *Allow your interest to show.* When viewing others' profiles, make sure your settings enable them to see you have viewed their profile. As their activity shows up in your feed, interact with them by liking, commenting, and sharing.... without being patronizing. If the person sees you have viewed their profile and recognizes your name from interacting with their content, they could follow up with you by making a connection request. If not, continue to interact with them from afar until you are comfortable requesting to connect.

- *Invite to connect.* After a period of time in which you have followed a user and interacted with them and their content, you have earned permission to ask to connect. Be sure to explain why you want to connect; what value would you bring to the person? Focus on the benefit of connecting, not that you are looking for a job and hope they can help.

The actions recommended above are not guaranteed to work. Some people, even some of your first-degree connections, will be unwilling to help. Do not let their inaction discourage you. They likely have a reason for not being a resource, but others in your network are going to be willing to help you.

Act on It

Dig your well before you are thirsty. You may not be searching for a job now, but you could find yourself in that situation in the future. The time is now to network for your next opportunity.

- Add five new connections this week. Begin by reviewing People You May Know in the My Network section. You likely have acquaintances, friends, and colleagues with whom you are not connected on LinkedIn but should be.

- Follow five people you do not know but with whom you would like to connect. Their activity will begin appearing in your feed. Make a point to interact with them by liking, sharing, and commenting on their activity. Doing so will put you on their radar. Once they are aware of you, the foundation is laid for eventually making a connection request.

Conclusion

Why do I feel like I am not all set on LinkedIn?

After sharing 25 different ways of enhancing your LinkedIn presence, I realize there is one point I failed to mention... but it is a big one. You will never be finished caring for your brand space on LinkedIn (I knew I was forgetting to tell you something, sorry). The reality is your professional identity is a brand, whether you want it to be or not. Marketers of a product brand will never be heard saying "We have a name, logo, website, and social media—great, we're done."

Like a product brand, your personal brand will never be all set. You will find that there is always work to be done to remain current, fresh, and relevant. That work includes remaining engaged with your network of connections on LinkedIn. Do not dread the challenge. Instead, think of it as an opportunity to build on the work you have put into your brand and help it grow.

It Is You but not about You

One more consideration to never lose sight of as you tend to your brand on LinkedIn: Do not make it about you; make it about the value you offer to others. This mindset is strange because after all, you are managing *your* personal brand. However, I again draw an analogy with great product brands. The most admired brands do not hold that status because the product maker boasts of its awesomeness. Great brands are held in high regard because customers and others appreciate the benefits received from the product. Similarly, your personal brand will not be distinctive because you are an amazing person (even though you are). Your brand will be distinctive because of the amazing ways you help and serve others.

Thank you for taking a journey through LinkedIn with me. I posed many questions and tried to answer them fully yet succinctly. It is my hope you have found the suggestions and best practices shared helpful to enhancing your LinkedIn experience. Keep in mind that there are other aspects of using LinkedIn not even covered in this book. Among the other uses of LinkedIn that warrant a deeper dive are using it as a sales channel and executing ad campaigns to reach and grow your audience.

Most of all, enjoy using LinkedIn. It can be an effective channel for your personal brand. Like any other marketing initiative, results depend on the investment, mainly of your time, that you make. I hope to cross paths with you on LinkedIn. Feel free to connect... just be sure to tailor the connection request.

About the Author

Donald P. Roy, Ph.D.

Donald P. (Don) Roy is professor of marketing at Middle Tennessee State University. Don has enjoyed a marketing career spanning over 30 years, even longer if you count his paper route in middle school.

After graduating from Mississippi State University with a degree in marketing, Don began his marketing career with stints in department store management and consumer packaged goods sales over a 10-year period. While completing an MBA at Mississippi College, Don decided to follow in the footsteps of professors that influenced him during his graduate program and become a college professor. He graduated with a Ph.D. from the University of Memphis in 2000.

Preparing the next generation of marketing professionals motivated Don to become a professor, and he has relished the chance to train future marketers over the past two decades. He has received teaching awards from the Marketing Management Association (Master Teacher Award) and Middle Tennessee State University (Outstanding Teacher Award).

Don has merged two of his professional passions—branding and mentoring—in his research into personal branding. His expertise includes using online communication channels for personal branding. He has made numerous presentations on using LinkedIn and other social media for personal branding.

Don and his wife, Sara, live in Murfreesboro, Tennessee and have three sons.

You can find Don online at http://donaldproy.com and on Twitter (@Don_Roy).

Don't forget LinkedIn! You can find Don on LinkedIn at https://www.linkedin.com/in/donroy/.

www.ingramcontent.com/pod-product-compliance
Lightning Source LLC
Chambersburg PA
CBHW070552220526
45467CB00003B/1180